Be the best
DANCE CAPTAIN
on Broadway

By Jennie Ford

Copyright © 2016 by Jennie Ford
All rights reserved.

Printed by CreateSpace

Available at www.CreateSpace.com/6368046
Amazon.com and other retail outlets.

Dedication

To every dance captain. The work never stops!

Author's Acknowledgements

Many thanks to all who have helped turn this book into reality. I would like to thank Steve Hanneman, Johnny Stellard, Gia Mongell, Carol McLaren, and Ron Ford, who helped edit it! "Merçi" to Camille Bertrand for her artistic talents and the endless hours spent entertaining my daughter during the process. Kudos to Gemi for introducing me to InDesign. Much thanks to all those who responded to "what makes a great dance captain". Thank you to all involved in *Evita*: Rob Ashford, Michael Grandage, Kristen Blodgette, stage management, the cast, the producers, the crew, and the gang at Bespoke Theatricals. I would be amiss not to mention my supportive family from the small town of Humboldt, Saskatchewan, who made me believe I could do anything I wanted with my life!

I have always wanted to give back to the Broadway community that has been so good to me. I love being a mentor and I thrive on seeing performers be the best they can be. It's been a year in the making, but there is finally a "how-to" book for dance captains! I couldn't be more excited about it!

Table of Contents

Preface 1

Buddy, the Worker Bee 2

Introduction 3

Chapter 1: What is a Dance Captain? 5
    When is a dance captain hired? 5
    The duties of a dance captain 6
    The expectations of a dance captain 11
    How much does a dance captain get paid? 12

Chapter 2: Job Titles and Hierarchy of a Broadway Musical ... 13
    Who is in charge of what? 14
    The importance of maintaining the "creative" team's vision 15

Chapter 3: Job Titles and Job Functions 19
    Job functions of coworkers 19
    The difference between a swing and an understudy 21
    The difference between a swing and a stand-by 21
    The difference between an understudy and a stand-by 21
    Different types of swings 22
    When do swings, understudies and stand-by's perform? 24

Chapter 4: Dance Captains and Swings 27
    Building the relationship between swings and dance captains ... 28
    Asking for help 29

Chapter 5: Dance Captains and Stage Managers 31
    Dividing responsibilities 32
    Working with different personalities 33
    Props and backstage business 34

Chapter 6: Offstage and Onstage Dance Captains 35
    The pros and cons..35

Chapter 7: Dance Captains and Choreographers 37
    Which dance captain for which choreographer?.............. 37
    What if I don't like how a choreographer is treating me?....41
    How to handle conflict.. 41
    When to contact the choreographer 42
    Does being a dance captain make you a better choreographer?. 44

Chapter 8: Taking and Giving Notes 45
    Dealing with different personalities 48
    When to give notes.. 51
    Ways to give notes...53

Chapter 9: Making a Show Bible 55
    What is a show bible 55
    What to include in the bible 57
        Charts... 57
        Staging notes 72
        Choreography 75
        Tracking sheets for each actor 80
    Stage Write 84
    Staging Score 88
    Using photos, video and audio recordings for the bible....94

Chapter 10: Rehearsals 97
    Overtime 98
    Weekly rehearsals.. 99
        How to run a weekly rehearsal 100
    Put-ins 107
    Different types of put-ins.. 107
        For a replacement actor..108
        For and understudy or standy-by............................ 109
        For a swing.. ...110
    Brush up rehearsals 114
    Lift rehearsals 114
    Safety rehearsals 118
    Partnering rehearsals... 119
        When one partner blames the other 119

Chapter 11: Scheduling 121
    Keep a "running list" 121
    How to make a weekly schedule 122
    How to schedule a put-in 126
    How to schedule lift rehearsals 128

Chapter 12: Running Auditions 129
    The audition combination 131

Chapter 13: What to Expect when Actors Call Out 133
    Daily "in/out" sheet 133
    Cut tracks/combo tracks 135

Chapter 14: A Day in the Life of a Dance Captain 141

Chapter 15: What Broadway People say Makes the Best Dance Captain ... 145

Chapter 16: Balancing the Leadership Aspect of the Position 151

Chapter 17: Should I be a Dance Captain? 155
    What training do I need? 156
    Your life is the show 157
    Finding a support system 159

Chapter 18: Extras to Help You 161
    Quick rehearsal reference 161
    Swing chart 161
    Swing to-do list 163

Chapter 19: Practise Exercises 165
    Learning names quickly 165
    Eye for detail 168
    Giving notes 168
    Creating cut tracks 169
    Figuring out what swings need with little notice 169
    What would *you* do? 170

Chapter 20: Glossary of Theatre Terminology 173

Index 193

Book series

Be the best on Broadway
www.bethebestonbroadway.com

Preface

There are thousands of performing arts schools grooming students for Broadway. Broadway is revered as the pinnacle of every performer's career. It's the "Olympics" of our sport that we have trained and worked so hard for. Would you be confident if you received a Broadway contract that said you were going to be a swing, a dance captain or an understudy? Hopefully you would reply *"yes"*...after all, you have a college degree in the arts, right? These are fundamental jobs in every Broadway musical, so why aren't graduates prepared to do those jobs? The problem is there is "book knowledge" from school and "learned knowledge" from being on the job. This book series bridges the gap between the two.

Students are taught how to pick songs for the roles they are right for, how to perform them, how to study scripts, how to audition and how to show the best of themselves. They study the history of theatre and graduate with confidence that they can nail that audition and land a job. What happens when a talented performer actually books a job? What skill-set do they have to prepare them for the responsibilities that come along with performing under a union contract? It's a rude awakening for some performers to find out about 85% of Broadway performers are *not* principal performers. Even the small percentage of principals on Broadway are not always principals! Sometimes, throughout their careers, they are part of the chorus, an understudy, an alternate, a stand-by, or a swing. The career choices are endless on Broadway and the idea is to prepare yourself for all opportunities.

"Be the best on Broadway" is a how-to-series that will demystify and teach those who want a career on Broadway, no matter how much schooling you may (or may not) have. It is the book series of learned knowledge and is intended to be the "go-to" resource for all things Broadway. There is currently nothing like it. Each book is written by a Broadway professional with first-hand experience and is regarded as an expert. Each writer is respected by his/her peers for the work he/she contributes on a daily basis on Broadway. The series breaks down the different job particulars in depth and provides tangible Broadway show examples. The goal is to combine valuable insight and resources into one book series to strengthen the chance of success for those who have the Broadway dream!

Buddy, the Worker Bee

This is Buddy. He is known as the Broadway "worker bee", and he is here to guide you. He will give you some tips, stories, and tricks of the trade, so look for him throughout this book. Buddy knows what it means to work hard and be a part of a team. Broadway is no different!

From the Author

When I first started in this business, I was a swing and a dance captain on the 1st National Tour of *Ragtime*. It was an amazing experience but a lot of work. I loved my job, but there was no end to the work I could do to make myself better, the show better, my *show bible* better, my note-giving better, and so forth.

I was nicknamed the "worker bee" by my stage manager and it quickly filtered through the company. Before you knew it, everyone was calling me by that name. I started getting pins of bees, stickers of bees, and many other goodies! This is for all the "worker bees" on Broadway who constantly strive to be the best we can be.

Jennie Ford

Dance captain for: *Evita, Ragtime, The Music Man, All Shook Up, Leap of Faith.*

Introduction

This book will prove to be invaluable to dance captains as well as any performer who wants to learn through this special "lens"...the eye of a dance captain! This book looks at Broadway through the unique perspective of a dance captain. It is a job function on Broadway not widely written about or taught in schools. Until now, it's been every actor fending for themselves when they get offered a dance captain contract. I have been there! It took me years to figure out what works and what doesn't. I wish I'd had someone or some book to give me guidance at the beginning of my career.

Think of this book as a "book of secrets" to give you the chance to be an outstanding dance captain. There is nothing more rewarding than being recognized by your peers for doing your job well. The skills you need go beyond the talent required on Broadway. This book also deals with the interpersonal skills needed for a career on Broadway. "Talent" doesn't give you opportunities, relationships do! The tips in this book will make you stand out as a dance captain. The goal is not to just do it well, but to become "the best" at it!

This book is geared toward someone with a keen interest in theatre. Beginners may find some of the terms unfamiliar at first. The intermediate and advanced actor may know the terminology and are now ready to perfect the skill of dance captaining. It's a lot of valuable information to take in, so you may not be able to digest everything on the first read-through. The purpose of this book is two-fold. You should read it to familiarize yourself with the concepts and get an overview of the dance captain position, but you will also want it "by your side" as a quick-reference guide when you are on the job. The ultimate goal is to have it be the only book you will need to help you be the best dance captain on Broadway!

Throughout this book, you will read stories *about* dance captains and stories *written by* dance captains. A number of people chose to write their stories anonymously to protect themselves and the show they were working on. The purpose of these stories is not to "tell on people", but rather to learn the lessons of how dance captains affect the lives of so many actors in a show. Dance captains are a key factor for the morale of a company and can help dictate what kind of experience the rest of the company has doing a show.

"Someone took me aside and said he was really upset that I noted him on his 'attitude' and he hoped he never gave off bad energy. It took me a second to realize what he was talking about and then I could not stop laughing. He misunderstood my note on his '(leg position) attitude'.
- Sarah O'Gleby (Dance captain)

"One of my favorite things is working with all ranges of people; 8 to 68 years old, sensitive to tough. To make a company happy you must learn the details early, stick to the integrity of the piece and listen to all the sides of the story when dealing with a situation. Being a dance captain is a big job, so the extra effort to get details is crucial for the success you have with your company."
- Antoinette DiPetropolo (Dance captain)

CHAPTER 1

What is a Dance Captain?

A dance captain is the person who maintains the integrity of a show's choreography and/or musical staging on behalf of the choreographer. Along with the stage manager and the musical director, this person is also responsible for teaching swings, understudies, and replacements, making sure they are comfortable performing the roles they have to cover.

When is a Dance Captain hired?

A dance captain is required when a choreographer is hired to create choreography and/or musical staging. The Actors' Equity Association (AEA) Production Contract rule book states:

> *"A Dance Captain must be hired when there is movement of such a nature that the maintenance of its artistic quality, as originally staged, does not fall within the normal duties of a Stage Manager. The Stage Manager shall not serve as Dance Captain."*

You will find a dance captain in almost every Broadway musical. In larger shows, there may be *co-dance captains* or an *assistant dance captain* to help manage the workload. Dance captains are not required in plays on Broadway unless there is a choreographer hired.

Choreography is the sequence of steps and movements that create a dance. It specifies human movement in terms of space, musical timing and energy. The language that specifies the movement comes from the dance techniques of ballet, contemporary, jazz, hip hop, modern, folk, techno, tap, pedestrian movement or a combination of these.

Musical staging is when actors are *blocked* to move to a song versus a scene. The difference between musical staging and choreography is that musical staging does not contain intricate dance movements. A director or a choreographer can create musical staging. However, a choreographer may be asked to do musical staging when the director feels there is more movement needed to tell the story than he/she is trained to do.

The Duties of a Dance Captain

The general responsibility of the dance captain is to maintain the artistic standards of all choreography and/or musical staging in a production on behalf of the choreographer. The dance captain works in tandem with the stage manager and musical director in conveying and maintaining the intentions of the *creative team*. The *creative team* or *artistic staff* consists of the choreographer, director, writer, composer, lyricist, and others who create the show. Once the show is open, the creative team leaves and the dance captain, musical director and stage manager assume the responsibility of maintaining the show.

The duties of a dance captain can vary from show to show. It will depend on who else is hired to maintain the show with you. The number of people involved will determine what you will be responsible for and how you do your job.

Equity's Guidelines for Dance Captains:

Actors' Equity Association established guidelines in 1970 to assist dance captains. It has been revised and updated since then. It can be found online at www.actorsequity.org under the documents section.

> *"The Dance Captain is a member of the company who maintains the artistic standards of all choreography and/or musical staging in a production. The Dance Captain shall always work in tandem with the Stage Manager in conveying and maintaining the creative intentions of the Artistic Staff. The Advisory Committee on Chorus Affairs (ACCA), in conjunction with the Dance Captain Subcommittee, is issuing these suggested guidelines to assist the Dance Captains in their assigned position."*

"1. Maintaining Artistic Standards and Technique of Original Production

> a. Review musical staging and choreography, give notes and/or schedule brush-up rehearsals (in coordination with the Stage Manager). Maintain all musical staging and choreography in the original style, intent, technique and energy level. (Note: All rehearsals are called by the Stage Manager as per allotted hours set forth in the contract)."

You are responsible for teaching choreography and musical staging to swings, understudies and replacement actors.
Watch the show and give notes to the company as needed.
Ask the stage manger to schedule a brush up rehearsal with the full company or part of the company when you feel it's needed.

"b. Maintain original spacing and positions in musical numbers."

Write down (usually in a show bible) where everyone is placed in musical numbers. If someone is directed to be on "stage right 15 toeing the seam", you need to know that to maintain the show or teach swings, understudies and replacements,

"c. Make sure condition of stage, rehearsal and/or audition space is safe and suitable for musical staging and/or choreography for rehearsals and performances."

If you notice splinters, uneven surfaces or slippery dance surfaces, notify the stage manager. You want to make sure the dance surface is not dangerous for the dancers.

"d. Within a reasonable period of time after show is set, the Dance Captain shall learn all choreography and musical staging."

The show is now open and *frozen*. The choreography will not change.
Now you must learn everyone's choreography in the whole show so you can teach the understudies, swings and future replacements.

"e. In cases of complaints or differences of opinion between cast members concerning choreography and/or musical staging, the Dance Captain shall make the decision."

Let's say Sally and Joe are dance partners.
They disagree with the each other's counting when they partner.
You must clarify or make a decision on what the final counting should be.

"f. The Dance Captain may not be required to block non-musical scenes."

> The stage manger shares the duties of teaching the show.
> You are not responsible to teach the scenes to actors.
> You teach the parts that contain musical choreography or musical staging.

"2. Responsibilities to Understudies and Swings

a. Assist the Stage Manager and choreographer, or their assistants, in the assignment of understudies and swings for numbers and important bits of business in musical staging and/or choreography."

> Usually the choreographer and director decide on who will be the understudies and covers for specialties. Once they leave the show, the stage manager will consult with them or their assistants on any further assignments. You may be asked for your input or you could suggest an idea to the stage manager if you felt someone would be a good cover.

"b. See that understudies and swings are prepared to perform assignments in musical numbers."

> Check in with the swings and understudies to see what they know and then schedule rehearsal so you can teach them what they don't. They are never expected to know things by watching. They need to be taught by you and the stage manger.

"3. Responsibilities for Replacements

a. Audition replacement Actors in regards to musical staging and/or choreography when required."

> You may be asked to run auditions for the show.
> You will teach dance combinations to actors who come to the audition.

"b. Teach chorus or principal replacements choreography and staging of musical numbers."

> You will teach choreography and musical staging to
> the new people who come into the show.

"c. Rehearse replacement with cast members involved in musical numbers prior to their first performance."

> You will rehearse the new actors with the existing company before their first show in front of an audience. It will likely be by scheduling a put-in and perhaps some individual partnering too.

"d. Apprise Actors of possible technical problems they may encounter, such as quick change set-ups, involvement with set changes or use of props in coordination and cooperation with Stage Manager."

> You, along with the stage manager, will tell the replacement actor where they quick change backstage, where they find their props, and other backstage business that affects their show or may be problematic.

"4. Daily Duties

a. Check with Stage Manager no later than half-hour to determine if any absences are anticipated."

> The latest you can be at the theatre is the *half hour call*. However, a dance captain rarely shows up to the theatre that late. You will have other duties, like giving notes, that bring you to the theatre about 45 to 75 minutes before show time.
>
> You will get a call from stage management long before half-hour if anyone is expected to be out of the show. It's a good thing to check in with the stage manager when you come to the theatre in case there are any questions about scheduling, rehearsing, or anything the stage manager needs to co-ordinate with you.

"b. In case of absence, in cooperation and coordination with Stage Manager:
(1) Inform understudy and/or swing concerned.
(2) Inform entire company of changes as soon as possible.
(3) Rehearse replacement with partners if lifts are required, and/or if other pieces of physical staging require rehearsal to ensure safety."

> The stage manager is the one who tells the swing or understudy if they are going on. The stage manager will also notify the full company. If there are things you need to rehearse, like lifts, then let the stage manger know so he/she can schedule it. You need to be present to run those rehearsals. If there are any changes that affect any particular actor in the show, you are responsible for notifying him/her.

"c. In case of principal's absence - in conjunction with Stage Manager - rehearse Actors involved with understudy if necessary or desired by Actor or Stage Managers."

If a principal is out and an understudy is going on, ask the understudy what he/she needs. Tell the stage manager what you need so he/she can schedule it. Then you will run any rehearsals they may need for lifts or choreography.

"d. If due to emergency someone other than understudy and/or swing has to perform, see that they are prepared as well as time will allow."

If someone gets asked to do something they weren't expecting because of an emergency, make sure you teach them what they need to know as best you can before they have to go on.

For example: If a snow storm hit that didn't allow actors to get to the theatre, another actor may be asked to fill in for an emergency. It may be something like doing a dance lift they've never done before, moving a chair they normally don't, singing a line they've never done, or moving a set piece they are not familiar with.

"e. Maintain record of all assignments and personnel, and note any changes therein."

The stage manager is the one who keeps a list of the understudies and who covers what parts. It's a good idea though for you to have a copy of that information too.

"f. Inform Stage Manager of all extra duties or changes being made so that money due is recorded."

The stage manager is the person who reports extra duties, such as set moves or having to cover a part or specialty that they don't normally. You are free to double check with the stage manager to make sure it was noted that an actor is due money, but it's not really expected of you.

"5. Dance Notebook
a. The Dance Captain is not required to create a dance notebook (i.e. stage diagrams, choreographic notation, etc.)."

The reason this guideline exists is because everyone does their dance captain job differently. There currently is no standard on how to make a show bible. Actors' Equity didn't think it should be expected if it was not part of the way a dance captain chose to do his/her job. However, there is rarely a Broadway show that doesn't have a bible of some sort. It's usually needed for maintaining the original spacing.

"6. AEA Council maintains the right to change, alter, or modify the above."

These are the guidelines the Council of Equity agreed upon the last time it revised this document in 2001. Council maintains the right to modify it in the future.

"The Dance Captain's hours shall not exceed the maximum number of rehearsal hours permitted by the applicable contract. All contract provisions for breaks and rest periods (including turnaround) shall apply. Please advise your Stage Manager when overtime is anticipated, and report all overtime to Stage Manager, and Deputy (if applicable)."

Dance captains can rehearse up to 12 hours a week without payment. If you work on the *day off* or the *day after the day off*, you will receive overtime but those hours won't count towards your 12 hours per week. The amount of overtime depends on what you are doing those days. If you rehearse during a show, those hours between *half hour* and the end of the show also do not count towards the 12 hours. You are entitled to the same breaks and rest periods as every other actor.

"If you have any questions, or need further information, please contact your Equity Business Representative.   revised 2/20/01"

There is a staff person at Equity assigned to every Broadway show. He/she is called your *Equity business rep*. You can always ask your show's deputy who the business rep is or you can call Equity and ask for the business rep for your show. Feel free to talk to your business rep anytime about questions relating to you personally as the dance captain. You don't have to go through the deputy.

The Expectations of a Dance Captain:

- Take notes during the show and giving them to actors.
- Make a *show bible*, although it is not required.
- Run weekly rehearsals for swings, understudies and new cast members.
- Help stage management schedule rehearsals.
- Create cut-tracks as needed.
- Run auditions for the show.
- Possibly being involved in preproduction (it's usually separate from your AEA contract and each choreographer does it differently).

How much does a Dance Captain get paid?

Actors' Equity Association (AEA) is the union that represents theatre actors and stage managers. It bargains with the producers to create the terms of each *Equity contract*. The Production Contract governs all Broadway theatre. The contract is renegotiated every 3 or 4 years and the contract changes each time. There may or may not be changes made to the salary or dance captain rules. The most up-to-date information about the Production Contract can be found at www.actorsequity.org. It is listed under "document library", then "agreements", then "Production Rulebook". There are two Production Rulebooks; one for League Producers and one for Disney Theatrical Productions. (Unless you are in a Disney show, you are governed by the League Producer's rulebook)

In the current Actors' Equity Association (AEA) Production Contract, a dance captain receives not less than an additional 20% of *actor minimum salary*. *Actor minimum salary* is negotiated by AEA and can change every year of the contract. For example, the actor's *weekly* minimum salary was $1917 as of September 28, 2015. (It often changes yearly.) So in that contract year, a dance captain would make at least $383.40/week in addition to their contractual salary. Dance captains are also entitled to overtime pay when applicable. Such times include running an audition on the day off, rehearsing on the day after the day off, and rehearsing more hours than allowed in the Production Contract.

A *co-dance captain* would be contracted at the same rate of 20%. An *assistant dance captain* gets no less than an additional 10% of actor minimum salary. Using the same example above, an assistant dance captain would make $191.70/week in addition to their contractual salary. (Even though an assistant dance captain makes less money, there is no difference in the duties that can be expected.)

> TIP:
> *Being a dance captain will never be your only duty! An actor is assigned to dance captain duties on top of his/her other jobs in a show. An actor could be a swing, an understudy, or onstage in the chorus as well as being a dance captain at the same time. We will talk more about this in future chapters.*

CHAPTER 2

Job Titles and Hierarchy of a Broadway Musical

There may be other job titles on your production and you want to know where you, the dance captain, are in rank. Not all the following positions exist in every show, but if these titles do appear, this is the ranking.

CHOREOGRAPHER	*DIRECTOR*	*COMPOSER/ LYRICIST*
Associate Choreographer	Associate Director	Musical Supervisor
Assistant Choreographer	Assistant Director	Musical Director/Conductor
Dance Supervisor	Production Supervisor	Associate Musical Director
Resident Choreographer	Resident Director	Assistant Musical Director
Dance Captain	Stage Manager	
Assistant Dance Captain	Assistant Stage Manager	

Usually the choreographer will have an associate and/or assistant while they are putting up a show. Once the show is open, they will leave. The choreographer or producers may decide to hire someone, other than a dance captain, to maintain the choreography for the remainder of the show's run. That position might be called a *dance supervisor* or a *resident choreographer*. This person would be hired full time or part time to maintain the show. You would report to him or her and assist in maintaining the show. If there is no such position on your show, then you are the direct representative on behalf of the choreographer.

Similarly, the director may have an associate and/or assistant. This person is called a *production supervisor* or a *resident director*. The stage manager would report to him or her and assist in maintaining the show. If there is no such position, then the stage manager is the direct representative on behalf of the director.

Either the *musical supervisor* or the *musical conductor* will be in charge of teaching the music after opening.

Who is in charge of what?

The person in charge of music, choreography and direction is different for every show. Take a look at your specific show to see what "positions" will be involved after opening night. The titles will be written in the Playbill or *billed* a certain way on the poster and online (IBDB or your show's website). This will tell you who will be in charge of each department. If it's unclear, you could always ask the stage manager and see who will be staying on after the show opens and what their "titles" are.

There are *many* shows that have the dance captain, along with the stage manager and musical director, in charge of teaching the show. It's best to have a conversation with your stage manager (or person in charge of teaching direction and staging) early in the process to identify the numbers you are responsible for. Some musical numbers or scenes may have both choreography and scene work. It may be created with the choreographer and the director working in tandem. Some musical staging done by the director may be too complicated for the stage manager to teach and it would become your responsibility even if the director did it. It's important to know who is responsible for teaching those numbers, or parts of the numbers, so neither of you are put on the spot in front of the company.

> TIP:
> *Sit down with your stage manager early on, so you know what you are expected to teach. Avoid arriving at rehearsal to find out the stage manager thought you were teaching something you didn't expect. (see more in chapter 6)*

The stage manager and the dance captain end up working closely together for the remainder of a show's run, just like the choreographer and the director did in creating the show.

The importance of maintaining the Creative Team's vision

The company may be doing it's 600th show, but most of the audience is seeing it for the first time. The show will affect each audience member differently. The show was created to tell the story in a specific way and it's your job to protect the integrity of the original vision. For the benefit of every "theater go-er", you continue to give notes to actors, and encourage actors to refrain from "fooling around". (if they become bored or discouraged)

Here is what some Broadway choreographers have to say about the importance of dance captains:

> Jerry Mitchell says, "To be a STAR onstage, you cannot perform and watch yourself at the same time. The dance captain (or associate) becomes the eyes, ears, heart and soul of the choreographer every night when a show is running. All of the actors, dancers, singers and triple threats I have had the joy to work with are 'FULLOUT'! To be truly 'FULLOUT', you need to be in the moment as a performer. The dance captain or associate is out front watching those 'FULLOUT' performances to keep the ORIGINAL step, idea and concept ALIVE in every performance. They are there to HELP the performer. Actors should use the dance captain's talent and expertise to their advantage. When the performance gets away from the original intention of the STORY BEING TOLD, the 'eyes out front' are the eyes to trust. That is why MY dance captains and associates are so important to me. They are there every night maintaining the ORIGINAL story being told and helping everyone stay true to that ORIGINAL intention."
> - Tony Award winning choreographer/Director, (Hairspray, Legally Blonde, Gotta Dance, On Your Feet, Kinky Boots, You're a Good Man, Charlie Brown, The Full Monty, The Rocky Horror Show, Imaginary Friends, Never Gonna Dance, La Cage aux Folles, Dirty Rotten Scoundrels, Catch Me If You Can,)

Susan Stroman says, "My dance captains are very important to me. They have some of the sharpest and quickest minds in the business. I always prefer to have my dance captains with me during preproduction whenever I'm creating something new. This is the moment for them to understand why I've created something in a particular way, to see where those ideas and motivations have come from. I expect them to be able to pay attention to how the show is created and absorb all that is happening around them. That's crucial because not only will they be maintaining it every night, but very possibly they will be recreating it all over the world."

> - Tony Award winning director and choreographer, *(Bullets Over Broadway, Big Fish, The Scottsboro Boys, Young Frankenstein, The Frogs, Oklahoma!, Thou Shalt Not, The Producers, Contact, The Music Man, Steel Pier, Big, Show Boat, Crazy For You, Picnic)*

Lorin Latarro says, "My dance captain at *Waitress* is my lifeline. I hired him because he is smart, organized and cares deeply about the integrity of our show. I asked our dance captain to write everything down - not just formations and numbers and dance steps, but most importantly, intention and genesis of ideas. The WHY you do the step is as important as HOW you do the step. Each person onstage must embody the big idea of the show and inhabit the same world. As new actors come into *Waitress* they don't have the benefit of six weeks of rehearsal and jelling with the company. The dance captain has to impart as much of that information and experience to the new cast members. The dance captain also has to maintain the perfect balance onstage of too much or too little. Actors get bored or add little things. My dance captain has to see the show through the prism of my eyes and make real time decisions about what should stay and what should go. Lastly, being a dance captain helps that person become a better actor and leader by seeing the big picture and leading peers. It is personally beneficial in so many ways for a career in show biz. It is a title I reserve for intelligent, caring artists who have the ability to understand intention and can articulate my ideas...not for the faint of heart or ego driven person."

> - Choreographer, *(Waitress, Scandalous)* and Associate choreographer, *(The Curious Incident of the Dog in the Night-Time, Hands on a Hardbody, American Idiot)*

Christopher Wheeldon says, "The dance captains are often the unsung heros. For *An American in Paris*, the dance captain (along with the associates) have to teach the new actors coming into the show and maintain the integrity of the choreography. Not just steps, but style and intention! They are my eyes and ears when I'm away, which is most of the time. They are in charge of keeping it 'Wheeldon'!"

> - Tony Award winning choreographer, *(An American in Paris, Sweet Smell of Success)*

Sergio Trujillo says, "I am extremely selective about who I choose to be the dance captain on any of my shows. It is very important to me that my vision be maintained with the integrity it was created with. Most of my dance captains are dancers who have worked with me before. Some of them have been part of my pre-production team. By being part of my creative process they understand where the movement comes from, why it was created, what is behind each choreographic moment and so on."

<small>- Tony Award nominated and Olivier Award winning choreographer, *(On Your Feet!, Hands on a Hard Body, Leap of Faith, The Addams Family, Memphis, Next To Normal, Guys and Dolls, Jersey Boys, All Shook Up)*</small>

"Once, as an onstage dance captain, during a number I saw someone fall out of the corner of my eye but couldn't tell who it was. When we hit the final pose, I saw that we were missing someone and I knew immediately who it was. I exited the stage for a costume change, which I had about 5 minutes for, and said to myself 'don't forget to do your track!' All I wanted to do was see how she was and figure out if she could complete the show. I did my costume change at lightning speed so I knew I would be ready to make my next entrance before handing the situation. I knew that if I didn't change first, I may not make my next entrance and it would just be a domino effect because I had vocal solos in the next scene. She decided she was able to complete the rest of the show slightly modified because we were halfway through act two. We would re-evaluate later for the next day. It was a reminder to stay calm and breathe while assessing a situation so you don't fabricate an emergency that wasn't there in the first place."

- Johnny Stellard (*EVITA, Anastasia*)

CHAPTER 3

Job Titles and Job Functions

You will be working with a number of people with various job titles and job functions. You need to be familiar with those titles and functions. As a dance captain, you will be responsible for helping teach swings and understudies as well as giving notes on the roles and tracks they perform.

Job Functions of coworkers:

A *dance supervisor* is someone who represents the choreographer. This position is not common. If there is a dance supervisor, he/she is "above" the resident choreographer and may or may not remain with the show after opening. If there are multiple companies of the same show, this person would travel to teach and maintain the choreography in *all* companies of the show.

A *resident choreographer* is also someone who represents the choreographer and stays after opening night. This person is your immediate supervisor who would let you know what your specific duties are. You will share duties with this person and those can differ from show to show. You will likely share note-taking, note-giving, teaching and running auditions.

TIP:
You may have both a dance supervisor AND a resident choreographer. The difference is the "resident" stays with one show and the "supervisor" oversees all productions of the show. (tours, Broadway, abroad)

A *resident director* is someone who represents the director after opening night. This person would teach all the directional intention and staging for the show. You would work in tandem with this person if this position exists.

The *stage manager* is the person who maintains the prompt book/calling script and is hired to *call* the show. This means he/she calls all the cues over the headsets to the crew for lights, scenery and automation during the show. There will be one production stage manager, also known as a PSM and many assistant stage managers (ASM) to help. They will organize the daily schedules, help run rehearsals, teach staging, manage props, manage personnel, and oversee set moves and scenery. They also uphold the union rules by keeping track of rehearsal hours and break times.

The *musical supervisor* is the person in charge of the overall music department. He/she may or may not be at the show on a regular basis.

The *musical director* is the person in charge of the orchestra who will be the regular conductor of the show. This person will likely be the one who teaches the music to swings and understudies if the musical supervisor is not with the show full-time. The associate and assistant musical directors will be in the orchestra and eventually conduct once in a while. The associate or assistant may also be asked to teach the music for the show.

A *stand-by* is an actor hired on a principal contract to cover one or two of the lead principals.

An *alternate* is an actor hired to regularly perform a leading role once or twice a week. This person may be on a principal contract, similar to a *stand-by*, but is assured to perform a certain number of shows per week. An alternate could also be an understudy in the chorus who is guaranteed to perform a certain number of shows per week.

A *swing* is a member of the chorus who covers other chorus tracks in the show. There are many types of swings: full swing, partial (*internal*) swing, vacation swing and universal swing.

An *understudy* is an actor (usually a member of the chorus) who covers a principal role in the show.

TIP:
You will be working closely with the swings, understudies, alternates and stand-by's. Understanding what they do will gain their respect.

What is the difference between a swing and an understudy?

> A swing is a chorus member who covers chorus parts.
> An understudy is a chorus member who covers principal parts.

A person can be a swing and an understudy on the same show if they cover both chorus and principal parts.

What is the difference between a swing and a stand-by?

> A swing is a chorus member who covers chorus parts.
> A stand-by is a principal member who covers a principal part.

Both positions are hired as part of the *offstage cast* for a show. They only perform when someone is out of the show. A swing is hired on a chorus contract and covers multiple chorus tracks. A stand-by is hired on a principal contract and covers one or two principals.

What is the difference between an understudy and a stand-by?

> An understudy is a chorus member who covers a principal part.
> A stand-by is a principal member who covers a principal part.

Both cover principal parts. The understudy is usually a member of the chorus and has his/her own track or duties to do in the show. A stand-by is offstage and does not have his/her own track. A stand-by would go on for the principal role before an understudy would.

What is the difference between an alternate and a stand-by?

> An alternate covers a principal part and is guaranteed to perform regularly.
> A stand-by covers a principal part but is *not* guaranteed to perform.

The remainder of the chapter will explore in depth these job functions and how they are used in a typical Broadway show.

Different types of Swings:

A FULL swing, most commonly used, is a *non-performing* member of the chorus who learns the tracks of the *performing* members of the chorus. He/she performs when a chorus member is absent.

A PARTIAL swing is a person in the *performing* chorus who learns the tracks of the other *performing* chorus members for a specific "musical number" or scene. For example: if someone was hurt during a scene, the partial swing (who is already in the show) would be in wig and costume and be able to step into any chorus track quickly for the next number.

A VACATION swing is a person who is hired when an actor is out of the show for any number of reasons (vacation, injury, personal days). This person is hired on an "as-needed" basis. They are not full-time and may be asked to work in different companies of the same show, such as Broadway and/or National Tours.

A UNIVERSAL swing is a person who is hired by a producer when there are multiple companies of the same show. They are hired full time and would go from company to company if the shows were on tour and/or on Broadway. They can be asked to go wherever needed, which could take them out of New York City, the state, or the country.

Let's look at a typical cast of a Broadway show
and see how everything works.

For example:

The Broadway show *EVITA* had:

5 principals onstage
1 principal offstage (which is the *stand-by*)
24 onstage chorus (including 2 partial swings)
6 offstage chorus (including 4 full swings and 2 vacation swings)
No universal swings because there was only one company

Here is an example of a typical Broadway show breakdown for principals and chorus (showing who covers whom)

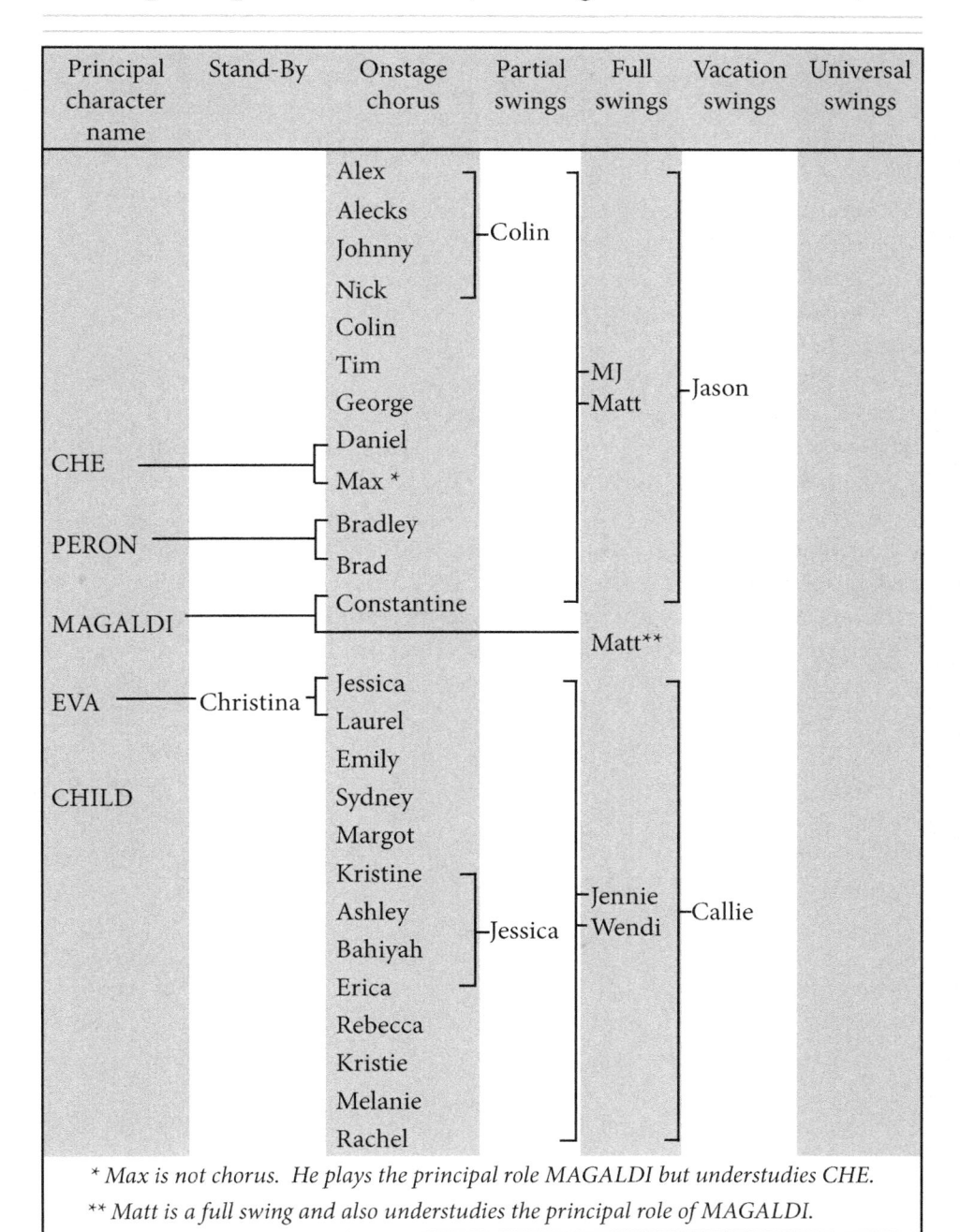

Principal character name	Stand-By	Onstage chorus	Partial swings	Full swings	Vacation swings	Universal swings
		Alex				
		Alecks				
		Johnny	Colin			
		Nick				
		Colin				
		Tim		MJ		
		George		Matt	Jason	
		Daniel				
CHE		Max *				
PERON		Bradley				
		Brad				
MAGALDI		Constantine				
				Matt**		
EVA	Christina	Jessica				
		Laurel				
		Emily				
		Sydney				
		Margot				
		Kristine				
		Ashley		Jennie		
CHILD		Bahiyah	Jessica	Wendi	Callie	
		Erica				
		Rebecca				
		Kristie				
		Melanie				
		Rachel				

* Max is not chorus. He plays the principal role MAGALDI but understudies CHE.

** Matt is a full swing and also understudies the principal role of MAGALDI.

When do swings, understudies and stand-by's perform?

There are many different scenarios and reasons why someone would have to perform for another actor. With a large cast and a long run, there are going to be shows when one or more cast members have to be out of the show.

- *Vacations*: Actors can take one week's vacation every 6 months.
- *Personal days*: Weddings, graduations, retirements.
- *Bereavement:* Someone in the family passes away.
- *Voice issues:* An actor loses his/her voice.
- *Jury duty:* An actor has to do jury duty.
- *Injuries*: Injuries can happen at the workplace or outside of the workplace.
- *Illness:* There are bound to be illnesses where an actor can't come in or doesn't come in to protect the cast from getting sick.
- *Contractual "outs":* Some actors may have contract clauses enabling them to film a TV show, record an album, do a concert date and so forth.
- *Swing outs:* Some shows rotate the swings regularly to keep them practising and minimize injury to the chorus caused by repetitive movements. There are instances where the understudies are swung out to watch a show or trail backstage to study the principal part they cover.

As the dance captain, you may be asked to help decide who will go on if an actor has to be out of the show. It's usually the stage manager who decides and comes up with a schedule for who is "out" and who is "in". The stage manager may ask the music and choreography departments to weigh in on the decisions.

If you are not a part of the decision making process, you can always take a look at the schedule and voice any concerns you have. The schedule can always be changed and it's important to make sure everyone scheduled to go on is prepared.

Here is an example of a Broadway show calendar. As you can see, the reason someone is out varies from personal days, vacation, jury duty, being swung out to watch the show and so forth.

Evita
Vacation / Personal Day Summary

MONTH AT A GLANCE
SUBJECT TO CHANGE

As of 1/17/2013

		# SHOWS	OUT	IN	REASON
Week Beginning	06/11/12				
Wednesday-Saturday	6/13-6/16	6	M. Passaro	L. Micklin	Vacation
Saturday eve	06/16/12	1	J. Athens	M. Ulreich	PD
Saturday	06/16/12	2	K. Covillo	J. Ford	PD
Week Beginning	06/18/12				
Monday	06/18/12	1	C. DeCicco	n/a	PD
Monday - Tuesday	6/18-6/19	2	L. Harris	J. Ford	PDs
Wednesday Matinee	06/20/12	1	M. von Essen	M. Wall	Jury Duty (TBD)
Thursday - Friday	6/21 - 6/22	2	A. Pevec	J. Garrett	PDs
Friday - Saturday	6/22 & 6/23	3	GL Andrews	M. Wall	Vacation (contractual)
Monday - Saturday	6/18-6/24	8	M. Passaro	Nolte/Micklin/Ulreich	Vacation (contractual)
Saturday	06/23/12	2	A. Amber	J. Ford	PD
Week Beginning	06/25/12				
Monday-Tuesday	6/25-6/26	2	M. Frank	I. Moner	PD
Monday - Saturday	6/25-7/1	8	K. Covillo	C. Carter	Vacation
Monday - Saturday	6/25-7/1	8	GL Andrews	M. Wall	Vacation (contractual)
Saturday	06/30/12	1	J. Athens	M. Ulreich	PD
Saturday	06/30/12	2	B. Mills	A. Grundy	PD
Saturday Evening	06/30/12	M. Frank's last show/I. Moner's last show			

In the chart above, it lists the cast and stage managers who will be out of the show for different reasons and who will be covering them. If someone only misses a couple of shows, then the company will not hire a vacation swing. In those instances, the full swing will always cover the person who is out of the show. A vacation swing will only be hired if someone is out for a week or more.

Which swing will be asked to perform?

Let's say Daniel is going on vacation for a week. The company will hire a vacation swing for the week Daniel is gone.

Daniel	Jason	MJ	Matt
Chorus	Vacation swing	Full swing	Full swing

All three of these swings know Daniel's track so who goes on?

Who goes on?

1) Management may choose to have Jason perform Daniel's track for the entire week and keep MJ and Matt available for other tracks.

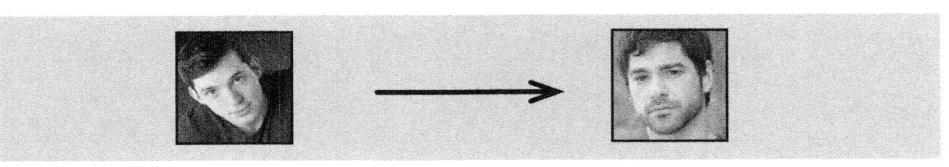

2) Management may choose to have Matt perform Daniel's track for the entire week and keep Jason and MJ available for other tracks.

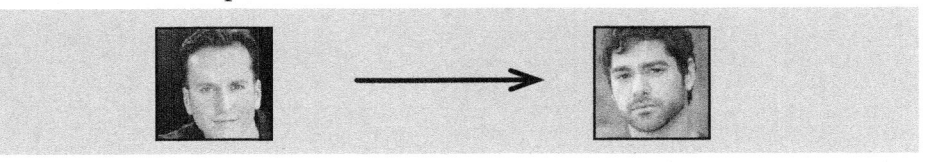

3) Management may choose to have MJ perform Daniel's track for the entire week and keep Jason and Matt available for other tracks.

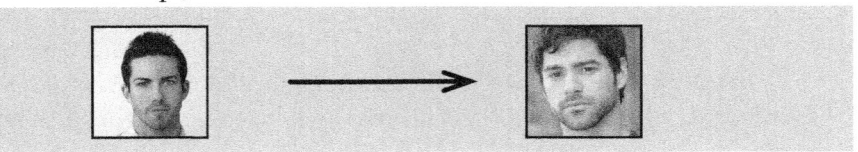

4) Management may choose a combination of swings to cover Daniel, allowing them to cover other people, who may be scheduled to miss that week.

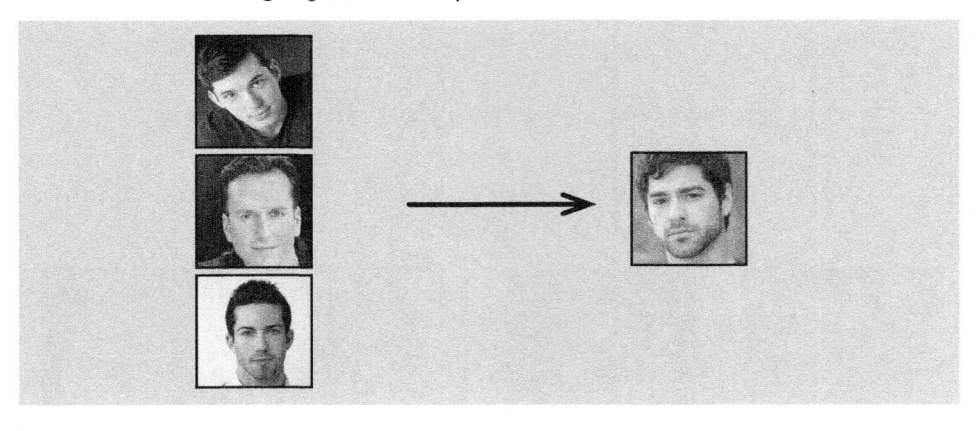

      Management decided to put Jason on for Daniel's entire vacation to keep it simple for the wardrobe, hair, and sound departments. There was an older gentlemen who sings bass in the cast, who had 2 personal days that week, so they left Matt available for that. There was also a dancer with featured partnering, who had 1 personal day, so they kept MJ available for that day.

CHAPTER 4

Dance Captains and Swings

The dance captain frequently is one of the swings. If the dance captain is not a swing, then he/she is onstage every show. It's very important for the dance captain to create a positive relationship with the swings. The dance captain is responsible for knowing where everyone is during the show and can help swings answer questions regarding the tracks they cover. Vice versa, swings can also be very helpful to the dance captain, providing details they gather regarding the tracks they cover.

The dance captain should be someone who the cast feels comfortable approaching if there are issues, such as choreography or musical staging, with fellow performers. If the dance captain doesn't know the answer, he/she should find it or find someone who has the answer.

The dance captain teaches the understudies and swings. When a new show starts rehearsals, it may be difficult for the dance captain to know everything. This is further complicated if he/she has their own track onstage and is not a swing. If the dance captain does not know a particular detail about the tracks he/she is teaching, the dance captain may ask the swings if they know. A swing's information and specificity is very useful to a dance captain.

Expectations of swings are numerous in the rehearsal process and it's a stressful time for them also. Give them compliments freely and often and see how eager they are to help you in return.

> *TIP:*
> *In no way are the swings responsible for teaching understudies or other swings. Teaching is the duty of the dance captain and stage manager. If swings want to offer valuable information, then let them. Show your appreciation and never expect it!*
>
> *Swings will likely teach, if asked, because you are in a "power position" with respect to them. However, they will start to feel resentful about it and lose respect for you. They will feel as if they are doing your duties.*

Building the relationship between swings and dance captain

The best way to build any relationship is by sharing "power" and not using a "superior" tone at work. There are many ways to help swings feel confident and appreciated. Showing great respect to the swings will be returned 10-fold. Here are a few ideas:

- Trouble shoot lift problems with a swing so they feel included.
- Compliment what they are doing *in front* of the company.
- Always acknowledge a swing when they go on, in the presence of the company and/or choreographer if possible.
- Compliment their note taking or the system they create for swinging.
- You have better access to charts and such, so be the leader of the group and see if you can help swings get what they need.
- You can be the messenger/conduit between *management*, *creatives*, and the swings.
- Check in with them often to see how they feel and if they need anything.

> *TIP:*
> *There are shows that have technically complex elements (such as sword fighting, pyrotechnics, boxing, roller skating, playing instruments, riding scooters) where actors are not used to doing these things on a regular basis. It adds an element of danger and risk. Extra care needs to be taken with the swings to make sure they are getting the information and practise needed to go into the show without hurting themselves or others.*

> **TIP:**
> *Some swings love to help if they feel appreciated. Others do not want to be bothered. Have a conversation with them individually to explain your challenges to determine if you can use them as a resource. Let them know you are always available to answer questions or concerns, review choreography, or help in anyway possible. Reassure them your goal is to support the swings and make sure they always feel comfortable.*

Asking for help

If you are an onstage dance captain, you have to rely on people to provide the information you need. This is most challenging in the beginning of a new show, when you are busy learning. There may be an assistant dance captain who can alleviate some of the challenges. If not, then it's important to create a good relationship with the swings and stage managers who will support you the most. The swings are a valuable resource but you have to make sure they don't feel like they are doing your job. It's a delicate balance between helping each other and mutual respect.

> *"I swung a show that was extremely technically challenging and dangerous. There was only one dance captain and one fight captain, who were both onstage performers. The swings were not allowed backstage during the tech process because it was too dangerous, although we were still expected to go on at a moment's notice if someone got hurt. The dance captain never once came to check on the swings. Because of the difficult technical aspects of our show, it was even more imperative that she check with us to see if we needed any information we couldn't get from watching. We were so concerned about everyone's safety if we went on and frankly, it was terrifying! We felt that no one was in our corner and taking up our concerns with management. It was a huge disservice to have our captains be onstage all the time and not communicate with us. I did not enjoy one minute of being a swing on that production because the dance captain failed to support us and help us do our jobs well."*
>
> — Anonymous swing

"We had a dance captain who was a fellow swing in our show. Even though our show had a resident choreographer, he decided it was better for him to sit out in the house and watch our rehearsals versus dance with us. He was a harsh judge and came across condescending. He was not encouraging about the good things we were doing, nor did he give us praise in rehearsals. He did not get up and partner with the girls to allow us to feel what it would be like to do lifts with another person. The morale was low because of him. He was such a critical 'judge and jury' who was seen as 'shirking his swing duties'. You can bet when he went on, he was judged by the cast. His numerous mistakes were not forgiven by the company. He did not give the company respect and did not gain it in return. He gained a lot of enemies which made his job even harder."

- Anonymous swing

TIP:
Be mindful of terminology you use that is potentially offensive to swings. Terms like "first cast", "second cast", or "moved *up* to a track" can be offensive. A swing is a specific job function of a show, not a "stepping stone". They actually get paid more than the onstage chorus and you should avoid language that could make them feel less valuable than other company members.

"It was the first understudy rehearsal for our new show. The dance captain was onstage and felt overwhelmed that he hadn't acquired all the knowledge needed to teach the understudies. I was a swing who also understudied. Each of the swings was assigned to an actor to teach them his/her understudy roles. I was a little taken aback because I was hoping to just practise what I was in charge of learning. I knew the role better than the dance captain, so I taught the understudy the role. After that, the understudy always came to me to ask questions and not the dance captain. I started getting funny 'vibes' from the dance captain that I was overstepping my boundaries. It made for a very awkward situation of knowing when I was needed and not needed. In either case, I only felt awkward and never appreciated".

- Anonymous swing

CHAPTER 5

Dance Captains and Stage Managers

The dance captain's role is to maintain the choreographic side of a show. The stage manager's role is to run the directorial and technical side of a show. Ultimately, the stage manager is in charge of the entire production. You will work in tandem with the stage manager to maintain the artistic standards set by the creative team.

The relationship between the dance captain and the stage manager is an important one. It's like a sibling relationship where you have to learn to get along as one happy family. It's important to create mutual respect for one another. You are somewhat in control of what a good, or bad, experience you may have during the run of a show.

> *TIP:*
> *Another reason for a positive discussion with your stage manager regarding division of teaching duties is it opens up the lines of communication and eliminates surprises in rehearsal.*

Dividing responsibilities:

> **TIP:**
> Charts and tables will soon become your organizational friend! A table can be made quickly and easily on many programs like "Microsoft Word", "Pages", and "Excel".

Here's an example from *EVITA* of the dance captain and the stage manager dividing teaching duties:

	Number	Direction	Dance Dept
1	Requiem/Circus	Che	Action of chorus and Eva/Mourning Tango
2	Junin'	All but...	Tango couple, Eva/Magaldi twirl
3	Buenos Aires	-	All
4	G. Night/Thank you	All	-
5	Art of the Possible	-	All
6	Charity concert	Scene stuff for all cast	All chorus dancing and Eva/Peron Tango
7	Another suitcase	All	Hooker business in catacombs
8	Peron's Flame	Peron/Eva stuff	All but...
9	A New Argentina		All
10	Balcony	Che/Eva and "heavy's business"	All chorus action
11	High Flying	Che	Eva change with the maids
12	Rainbow High/Tour	Che, Eva and Person business	All
13	Chorus Girl	All	-
14	Money	-	All
15	Santa Evita	All	lift (little girl onto shoulder)
16	Waltz	-	ALL
17	You Must Love Me	All	-
18	She's a Diamond	-	ALL
19	Dice are Rolling	All	-
20	Eva's Final Broadcast	Che, Eva, nurses, Peron business	All
21	Montage	-	All
22	Lament	Eva on balcony	All but...
23	Bows	All principals	All

As you see from the chart, there are places where the dance captain is responsible to teach the entire number to everyone in the cast, chorus and principals. There are some numbers the dance captain does not have to worry about at all. There are also numbers that "overlap". Both departments will teach a part of it, or know each other's parts, enabling them to teach well together.

There is much to learn and it will be beneficial to have this conversation with your stage manager to eliminate work for yourself. After this conversation, you can feel confident and not worry about learning certain numbers during the rehearsal process. You can focus on obtaining the other information instead.

Working with different personalities:

There may be times when you encounter stage management personalities that may not jive with your own. You have to find a way to relate to them so work doesn't drive you crazy. You have to teach them how to treat you and vice verse. The best tip is to get to know them on a more personal level. You want to develop trust, find out some commonalities, and give praise for the hard work they do. Both positions require copious hours of commitment and sometimes all you need is a little appreciation to "melt the ice".

Both the dance captain and the stage management positions are partially "managerial" jobs. You may find that a stage manager does things differently than you would. If you find yourself frustrated over it, then consider if it's really worth the anxiety and frustration. Is it a lesson that the stage manager has to learn in his/her career, or is it *your* lesson? How can you contribute to making the situation better? Relax more, use humor, let some control go?

TIP:
It's almost impossible to change someone so try to alleviate your stress by finding humor during those difficult moments and ask yourself "what is my lesson?"

Props and Backstage business

Nowhere is it written who is in charge of teaching the props and backstage business. Usually the stage managers have a grasp of what props are handled and where to get them from. However, they may not know all the details of how they are used in a number. Sometimes the dance captains teach prop handling and what goes on backstage with costume business. It will differ from show to show. Have this conversation with the stage manager to figure out who is expected to know what. You can always work in tandem to get the information if it feels overwhelming. The swings are also a great resource because they are looking at those specific details all the time too.

"I created a great relationship with the stage manager I was working with. The stage manager went on vacation for a week and the assistant stage manager took over. I was the swing and the dance captain and I was on for a role I hadn't done before. My family happened to be in town that week and I was performing in the show at night. I kept getting texts from the assistant stage manager during the show, asking me for various things he needed from me to make the schedule for next week; The running order of the put-in, an outline for lifts during the put-in, who would be needed for understudy rehearsal, if I could look over the vacation list, when we should do lift rehearsal, and so on. Then I got a text saying 'are you getting my texts?'. I was livid! At least wait until the show is over! Does he not realize how much he's asking of me? I got up at 5:30am and did all the scheduling and answered all his questions. It took me until 9:30am, 4 hours, to complete all he asked of me. It was a case of overcompensation because he wanted to do a good job while the stage manager was away. I finally had to go in the next day and explain what it felt like and how much time it took to answer all his questions that came at once. He didn't seem to understand. That is when I realized that I couldn't change that person's lack of comprehension and I had to just learn how to work with him. I would have to learn how to say 'What is most important to you? I have one hour to work on this, so I want to make sure I get you what you need because I won't be able to get it all done tonight.' I was teaching 4 hours a day, entertaining my out-of-town guests and then performing in the show. The assistant stage manager sat in the office during rehearsals, and the show, and caught up on the paperwork he wanted to. He was only looking at things from his point of view. He truly didn't understand or appreciate the scope of my job, and I had to learn not to get so upset about it. It was so ridiculous, but I had a choice. I could cry about it or laugh about it. I cried one night and then learned to laugh from then on."

- Annonymous dance captain

CHAPTER 6

Offstage and Onstage Dance Captains

There is a considerable difference between an *onstage* dance captain and an *offstage* dance captain. There are pros and cons to both positions. Most choreographers find the show benefits more from at least one offstage dance captain because it's easier to execute a dance captain's duties. It's not to say an onstage dance captain won't do as good of a job, it's just that it presents more challenges to get the job done.

An *Offstage* Dance Captain

This would be a swing who covers a number of tracks. He/she learns the choreography of the entire show to execute dance captain duties.

The "Pros":
1. Writing down information during rehearsals is easier when you don't have to be in one particular track the whole time.
2. You can sit in the audience often to watch and take notes.
3. You get to partner with many different people as a swing, so you really get to know what couples are doing.
4. You gain the respect of the company quickly if you are a good swing.
5. The company respects your notes and opinions because you perform many tracks and can relate to what they are going through.
6. It's easy to rehearse replacement actors during a show if you are not in the show.
7. You are free to be anywhere in the theatre during show time to

troubleshoot problems and seek answers to questions you have. (house, wings, cat walk, dressing room)
8. You don't have to perform every night, so you avoid the wear and tear that repetitive choreography can have on your body over time.
9. You have to learn many tracks as a swing so you are almost "half way there" with what you are required to know as a dance captain.

The "Cons":
1. You won't be performing every night, if that is something that means a lot to you.

An *Onstage* Dance Captain

This would be an actor who performs in his/her own track every show, while learning the rest of the show to execute dance captain duties.

The "Pros":
1. You can become very confident in performing your track and then use that information as a basis for other tracks you must learn.

The "Cons":
1. Writing information when you are rehearsing a new show is difficult.
2. Getting time to sit out in the audience and notate the show.
3. Knowing the intricacies of all the tracks because you are used to doing your own.
4. Finding time and opportunities to problem solve and answer questions while performing every show.
5. Gaining respect from fellow actors that you perform with every night who may feel you cannot relate to what they are going through.
6. Your body will be tired from teaching all day and performing the show.
7. Finding a way to learn other actors' choreography in order to teach someone when you are doing your own track every night.

TIP:
Don't "expect", but appreciate any help from others who will share information you need.

CHAPTER 7

Dance Captains and Choreographers

The relationship between a dance captain and a choreographer varies with each show. The needs and expectations of the choreographer are the determinants. It also depends on whether there is another person helping the choreographer (resident choreographer, associate or assistant). In cases where the choreographer has a helper, take time to observe how that person interacts with the choreographer. It will indicate how you, as the dance captain, need to "show up". You may be called upon immediately to help or you may be slowly integrated into the process while the choreographer gets to know and trust you.

Which Dance Captain for Which Choreographer?

Here are some examples of choreographers and what they may need from a dance captain to complement them:

Choreographer A:
- He does not count music and comes from a modern background.
- He just won the Tony Award last year for his first Broadway show so the producers expect great things.
- He likes to improvise on the spot and have someone remember what he did.
- He likes his movement free and not rigid.
- He likes to change and alter it every time he does it.

- He works with the actors and puts in steps they like also.
- He comes to rehearsal right at the start or sometimes late.

Dance Captain for A:
- Can pick up choreography quickly.
- Can adapt to changes easily.
- Great attitude to help actors who struggle with the constant changes.
- Someone who can let go of being so anal and "make friends with their eraser". (There will be constant changes and you will notate them)
- Someone who can count music and translate for teaching purposes.
- Someone who can keep calm under chaos and pressure.
- Someone with a good memory or note taking skills. With all the changes, there will likely be actors who forget the last version.
- Someone who is not afraid to make choreographic suggestions (verbally or physically) when he is open to suggestions to improve.
- Someone who is prepared to proceed if he doesn't show up in time. Perhaps leading a warm up with the cast or reviewing choreography as needed. (In no way are you going to be expected to choreograph just because the choreographer is late) You just have to show up as a leader.

Choreographer B:
- She is very specific about counts, steps and intentions.
- She comes from a musical theatre background of all-round jazz, tap, ballet, and gymnastics.
- She has been on Broadway for years, experiencing highs and lows throughout it.
- She likes to choreograph in isolation and then try it out on a few people in pre-production.
- Every step has been choreographed during pre-production and she knows exactly what it is when the full cast is called to rehearse.
- She likes someone else to teach the choreography as she watches.
- She never improvises and will never ask an actor to contribute a step.
- She likes things very clean and precise.
- She comes to rehearsal an hour early to prepare for the day.

Dance Captain for B:
- Someone who is very detail oriented.
- Someone who is clear and specific when teaching choreography.

- Someone who is well rounded in tap, jazz, ballet and even gymnastics, familiar with all the dance terms she uses.
- Someone who never offers choreographic advice (verbally or physically).
- Someone who has a very good eye for detail and can see minute differences as the performers execute the choreography.
- Someone who can take notes and give notes well to maintain the specificity throughout the run of the show.
- Someone who is early, warmed up, and ready to go when she needs you.
- Someone who is always prepared and organized.
- Someone who checks with the choreographer before cleaning any part of the choreography such as heads, hand positions, etc.

Choreographer C:

- He is highly regarded in the ballet world and works mostly with ballet terms.
- This is his first Broadway show and the pressure is on because the producers took a chance.
- In addition to ballet, he will have to choreograph tap and jazz numbers.
- He counts, but could change every time, depending on how he "feels" the music.
- He doesn't have much tolerance for singers who can't dance and makes it known.
- He seems to have his favorites and always puts them in the same places.
- Happy to come up with a "messy big picture" and have someone else clean up the details.

Dance Captain for C:

- Someone who really knows ballet terminology with basic knowledge of tap and jazz too.
- A calm and friendly personality, not adding stress to the choreographer.
- Someone who learns choreography quickly and can translate it into counts.
- Someone who accepts change and lets the choreographer be in charge at all times, while being a person he can rely on for counts.
- Someone who is a buffer for the cast, especially the ones who don't feel appreciated.

- Someone who can support the singers who need it and compliment them often, making them feel appreciated.
- Someone who recognizes the inequities of staging, yet does not bad mouth the choreographer. Instead, remains happy, helpful, humorous, and in turn, becomes a trusted sounding board for the cast.
- Someone decisive and confident when cleaning up the choreography, not checking in all the time with the choreographer.

As you see, the role of a dance captain can vary depending on the situation. During the course of your career, you will likely be a dance captain for all three of these personalities and more. The strongest skills you need are observation and adaptability.

Ultimately, the choreographer wants his/her show to look good while maintaining a happy company. They want the company to like and respect the dance captain. This way, the company will respect the notes given to them when the choreographer is not there. It's a trust game. If the choreographer trusts the dance captain, the dance captain builds trust within the company.

> TIP:
> *Clarify counts, spacing and movements while the choreographer is still there. Make hand grips "uniform" during rehearsal clean-ups. (Uniformity, where possible, helps the swings and understudies). When the company sees the choreographer interacting with you, they begin to trust you know the answer, when they come to you later.*

There may be many tests of trust too, from the choreographer. You need to be ready to soar through them.
Some examples include:
- Running a warm up if they ask you to bide time for them in rehearsal while they create choreography.
- Cleaning up choreography with the whole cast.
- Teaching the full company, in front of the choreographer.
- Helping a swing or understudy get ready to step in during rehearsals.
- Helping couples who are having trouble partnering so the choreographer doesn't have to take time away from rehearsal to do so.

It's important for you to know when uniformity may stifle the "freshness" of choreography. You may have to sacrifice moments of being "uniform" and let each dance couple have something that feels better to them. It's a balance. Be clear and consistent with what it is, "free" or "set".

What if I don't like how a choreographer is treating me?

There may be a few reasons why you feel mistreated:
1. They aren't "jelling" with you.
2. They don't know you or trust you enough yet.
3. They are acting how they normally do and you are particularly sensitive.
4. They are under a lot of stress at home or at work.
5. They are just having a bad day.
6. They could be struggling with any number of issues such as substance abuse or other health challenges.

How to handle conflict

The first thing you should do is "take a breath". Do not immediately confront the choreographer regarding your feelings, as valid as they may be. It's best to observe and see if the behavior persists over time. If you talk to the choreographer, it could help your relationship or backfire on you. When you chose to have the conversation with him or her, you want to be non-emotional, non-accusatory, well-spoken and know what you are asking for. You want to address this properly just like in any professional workplace.

1. Acknowledge your feelings and self articulate or seek advice from a close friend outside the show.
2. Observe and note when it happens. Does it occur all the time or particular times? What are you doing then?
3. Is this something you need to address in order to do your job? Can you manage for the time you have to work with the choreographer and still gain the respect of the company and stage management?
4. Is there someone in management you could have a confidential conversation with? Perhaps a trusted stage manager? Ask him/her what his/her perspective is or if they observe something you don't.

If you decide that it's worth a conversation with the choreographer:
1. Rehearse your conversation at home in front of the mirror or with a close friend.
2. Create a script that will help you stick with the facts and not let emotions cause you to say something you may regret.
3. Find a time when the choreographer is the least busy and/or stressed.
4. Advise him/her that you would like to have a moment to discuss something and ask him/her when it works for them. Make it a private conversation so he/she doesn't feel defensive or threatened.
5. Present it from your feelings verses his/her actions. "I may be oversensitive", " I want the best for the company", "I want to express how I have been feeling and the effects it has", "I wanted to make you aware and see if there's something I can do to help alleviate the situation".
6. Ask if there is anything you can do differently or better to help the situation or enhance the working relationship. You want the company to respect you when he/she leaves and they could help set the precedent and the tone for the rest of the run.

When to contact the choreographer

It is best to have a conversation with the choreographer to clarify the times he/she wants you to communicate. This will determine when he/she would like to hear from you and if he/she needs to be in touch on a regular basis. If yes, then keep the dialogue continuous between you and the choreographer once the *creatives* leave the show.

Do **not** call the choreographer when:
1. Too many actors are out of the show and you have to make cuts or split tracks
2. Minor injuries necessitating a choreographic adjustment for a show.

Some examples when you may want to consult with the choreographer are:
1. More serious injuries: If you find you have to make a choreographic adjustment for a series of shows, then you can consult with the choreographer. Inform him/her what the issue is, what you plan on doing and other possible suggestions you've thought of. Listen to his/her response. He/she will give you his/her blessing or offer alternative suggestions.

2. The show has been asked to perform a number on TV or live. The producers will likely contact the choreographer and have him/her involved. In the event they don't, and you are being asked all the questions, contact the choreographer to keep him/her involved. After all, it is his/her name being represented by the choreography.
3. When a choreographer asks you to, even on a regular basis. Perhaps the choreographer does not have a good relationship with the stage manager and doesn't trust he/she is including all the details in the show report.

> "I was dance captain for EVITA and one of the actors playing a leading role got injured playing softball. He was choreographed to rotate a bed with 3 other actors. He had to run onstage, grab one of the bed posts, and run around in a circle very fast to rotate the bed. The illusion was pretty magical because he was replacing another character during this rotation. From an audience's point of view, they were watching one character and in a blink of an eye, the scenery changed and they were watching another character. The actor pulled his groin quite badly. He felt he could perform all of his show except for running around the bed. I asked the other 3 actors involved, to try the bed spin without him before the show to see if they could manage. They said it was more difficult to maneuver but manageable.
>
> I felt comfortable with the decision to keep him in the show and alter the bed move for the show, or for the next few shows if needed. I checked in with him every day before the show and he would tell me he wasn't heeled enough and he wanted to continue the choreographic alteration. Finally after about two weeks, the stage manager and the resident director asked me if we could get the original move back into the show. When I approached the actor about going back to the original way, he explained that as the character, the President of Argentina, it always felt weird to run and maybe we could keep it this way. He felt very strongly about it and would be happy to talk to the choreographer and director about it.
>
> The director was asked his thoughts by the resident director. The director preferred to put it back to the original way because of the effect. That is when I knew I didn't have to make this decision alone. I called the choreographer to explain the situation and he made the final decision. It took pressure off me having to make the final and 'right decision'."
>
> - Jennie Ford

You don't have to make the final decision, just facilitate it! Everything shows up in the show report written by the stage manger. This report goes to producers, general managers and *creatives*. Don't let the choreographer be surprised. Let them hear it from you and allow them to continue to be involved and empowered.

Does being a dance captain make you a better choreographer?

There are dance captains who want to be choreographers and there are those who do not. Just because you have the skills to choreograph, does not mean you have the skills to be a great dance captain. Similarly, just because you are a great dance captain does not mean you will be a great choreographer. There are plenty of dance captains who have no desire to choreograph. The two roles are very different and each requires a different skill set.

A choreographer tells a story through song and dance and propels the story forward in each musical number. Not every dance captain can come up with original steps or effectively tell a story through dance. The role of being a dance captain *may* help someone be a better choreographer, but it definitely does not work for everyone.

The dance captains, who aspire to be choreographers, use the position as a chance to work with a choreographer in the beginning stages of mounting a show. They get to observe the choreographer's process. Each choreographer has a different way of doing things. Some choreographers involve the dance captain, along with the assistant and/or associate choreographer, in the pre-production process. Some choreographers will allow freedom of input or choreographic suggestions, and others prefer to do everything on his or her own.

There are aspects of the dance captain duties that prepare you to manage people more effectively and be more organized as a choreographer. Dance captains likely have organizational skills, teaching skills, personal skills, and are able to maintain the show. All these qualities help someone be a better choreographer.

"The most interesting part (of being a dance captain) is figuring out what the choreographer wants from you. Some don't want to be bothered by small details and want you to clean the choreography and make decisions. Some want you to note any questions and check in with them before locking things in. Talk to your choreographer, if you've never worked with them before, and find out what they want from their dance captain."

- Ariane Dolan (Dance Captain)

CHAPTER 8

Taking and Giving Notes

You come to the theatre 1.5 hours before show time to start giving notes.
You have at least 25 notes to give out.
You finish giving your notes for the show.
You tell the stage manager where you will be watching the show from.
You take your note pad to the house to watch the 8:00 pm show.
You write the notes without disturbing the patrons.
You come back at intermission to be available for actors.
You watch and notate the second act.

Many people associate taking and giving notes as one of the major functions of a dance captain. Although important, it is really a minor part of a dance captain's work load. The most important aspect of taking and giving notes is *how* you give the notes! It's easy to observe the show and write down what needs fixing. The skill of being a great dance captain has to do with how you relate to people while giving notes and corrections.

> TIP:
> *The most important aspect of taking and giving notes is how you give the notes! The skill of being a great dance captain has to do with how you relate with people!*

Here are examples of notes taken and how they may be given:

1. You notice that Judy is having a hard time with the choreography in one of the production numbers. You know she is self-conscious of her dancing so you have to approach her appropriately.

   Make sure you can speak with her privately. You don't need to pull her out of her dressing room because that could make her feel anxious. Just go up to her in the dressing room and speak softly and privately. Start by talking with her about something in her personal life to show you care about her, not just the show. Give her a compliment about something she is doing correct in the show. Mention you want to help her. Tell her she is doing a great job but you can help her make it even better. She will get it! She will appreciate how gently you bring it up. You offer to show her the steps and practise with her a few times. You can do it at her dressing table, in a hallway close by, or on the stage at a convenient time when she is there. She will likely not "nail it", but she will do it better each time and feel proud about it. Make sure to encourage her by giving her praise. Let a show or two go by to see what improvements she makes. If she's still having problems, go back again. Because her experience was positive the first time, she will be more open to trying it again.

> *TIP:*
> *You get more bees with honey! However, the "honey" has to be real and genuine or most performers will see through it!.*

For example, you could calmly and quietly say something like: "Hey Judy! (warm smile) How's your knee? I know it's been bothering you. You can't tell you're having problems with it during the show! If you need me to adjust anything that you think might cause a problem, let me know. .... I have a couple things from watching the show last night. First of all, you were incredible in the last scene. You made me cry and I have watched it 100 times before. ... I just wanted to clarify a difficult choreography section in one of the numbers. You are doing a good job and there are just a few things we can add to make it great." Then after she practises and does it, you can say, "Judy! That was awesome! I am going to have to start referring to you as *master* dancer!"

> *TIP:*
> *A note that is funny to one actor may be patronizing to another. Learn how to communicate with each individual person!*

2. You notice that Ralph is starting to exaggerate the choreography and is pulling focus from the scene. The intent of the choreographer was to have everyone dance as if they were underwater (slow, subtle, and complimentary to the main action of the scene).

   You know how much Ralph loves to dance. He was a principal dancer for the ballet, and he has a hard time wanting to dance the same as everyone else. He is exceptional, and it's hard not to watch him during the scene. He has won numerous dance awards, recognizing his abilities. He feels under-used in this show. It's important for you to approach him in a way that keeps him open and not defensive. Acknowledge his contribution to the show and how magnificent he looks doing it. Remind him that it would be okay if there wasn't a scene going on in front of him that the audience needs to understand. Find other places where he can feel free to express himself and not feel confined.

   For example, you could say something like:
   "I know you may not be able to help this, but all I want to watch in that scene is you. (using humor with a smile) I wish there wasn't a stupid scene going on at the same time! It's right on the edge of taking the audience out of the moment and I need you to pull some of your movements back just a bit. The moment when you are center and doing the kick is probably the most vulnerable moment for the scene. The turns you do to stage left are gorgeous; they just need to slow down a bit. The moment that you are doing the developé (dance term) is stunning and not in competition with the scene."

   There is another aspect of practicing how you deliver criticism; it is finding a way to deal with a wide range of personalities. You may easily deliver a note to one actor, then deliver the exact note in the same way to another actor, and have him/her "blow up". Welcome to the complexities of dealing with personalities!

Dealing with different personalities

It helps to remove your ego from the job and look at everything from a perspective other than your own. To you, it's easy to justify your notes are correct, believing every actor should take them because that's what would make the show look better. It's not about the notes; it's about people. You have to look at "personalities" in order to effectively give them notes.

Here are some personality factors that may affect how you approach various members of the company:

"Principal now chorus": One actor just finished being the lead in a Broadway show that closed. Now she is performing in the chorus and seems to have a personal issue with not being the lead.

"Principal now chorus, who doesn't dance": One actor was the lead singer in a Broadway show. Now he is in the chorus and expected to dance. He is very self-conscious and extremely concerned about making mistakes.

"Pregnant": One actor just found out she is pregnant after losing her last child at 2 months. She has only told you because she wants to continue dancing, but needs to be careful.

"Perfectionist": One actor is a perfectionist who hates feeling like he did something wrong. He hates notes and gets defensive about everything.

"Injured": One actor had a major previous injury that is now bothering her again. She is worried that she won't be able to continue performing the show but really needs the money.

"Choreographer/actor conflict": One of the lead actors did not have a good relationship with the choreographer and does not agree with many of the choreographer's decisions. Every note he gets seems to bring up an issue from the actor's stand point. He expects you to justify it as an actor.

"I used to...": One of the lead actresses did her role in a previous version of the show. She was working with a creative team that was fired and now has to do the same show with a different choreographer and director. She always compares what she did before to what she is doing now.

"Movie star": One of the lead actors is a famous movie star. He is the reason people buy tickets to the show. He is superstitious regarding his warm up before a show and never wants to be disturbed.

How do you manage these types of personalities?

One justification is "you have a job to do and who cares?" You are going to give them the notes however it comes out of your mouth, when it's convenient for you. You will get your job done, but you will not create a very happy work environment. It will quickly become an "unhappy family" and you will not have many allies.

This brings up the old question, "Do you want to be right or happy?". There is a way to be both, but you want to keep "happiness" as a top priority.

Tools for your "tool box" when giving notes:

- Mutual respect and trust
- Humor
- Lightness, love and laughter

You need to gain mutual trust and respect. You must respect where the performers come from and what they are going through. In return, they will give you respect. Start by having conversations with some actors one on one. Get to know who they are. Get them to see you as a friend. You will start to know them on a personal level. Acknowledge the good work they do, often. Everyone likes to hear a compliment. Do it genuinely though, not all the time, or it will seem false and they won't trust the compliments. If you give compliments while being particular and still pointing out where you could help them, they will trust your compliments.

Another tool to use is humor. Humor can break the tension and give people permission to laugh at themselves. The skill comes when you recognize when humor can be used. Some actors will respond well to it and others may find it condescending. Again, it's about "taking the temperature" of the person and learning how to best communicate with him or her.

We can get so wrapped up in thinking something is a "big deal". A choreographer may be stressing out and state something is "dire" to fix. Do what you can, but keep in the back of your mind that nothing is *really* that serious. (Death is a big deal! Is this person dying?) This is a show! Yes, it's important but put it in perspective. Do not over-react. Even in stressful situations, the best medicine is lightness, love and laughter. The company will be relieved to see your smiling face in the midst of chaos and frustration.

For example:

Using humor: "Principal now chorus, who doesn't dance": "I am really impressed with you! You are working hard and it shows. Pretty soon we are going to have to give you your own dance solo." Then he/she will usually smile or laugh and ask you to help them with parts of the choreography they haven't mastered yet. At times you don't even have to say the note. The actor already knows and volunteers their own flaws without you emphasizing them.

Have mutual respect and trust: "Pregnant" girl feels comfortable with doing her show, except for one lift she does with a guy where he is grabbing her stomach. She doesn't want anyone to know. You tell both actors that you notice the lift looks slightly different from the other couples and you would like to work on it when it's convenient for them. When they come to practise, you could say, "You are doing the proper grip, but for some reason it looks different. Every person's body is so different so I wanted to try a couple different grips with you to see if it works and still looks the same as the other couples". Then you can try his arm around her hip, butt, armpit and so forth. As long as the timing can remain the same, you can check in with the girl during the rehearsal and ask her if that feels good without blowing her secret.

> *TIP:*
> *Acknowledge the good work actors do, often. Everyone likes to hear a compliment. It makes it easier to hear criticism when you hear compliments. Do it genuinely though, not all the time, or it will seem false and they won't trust the compliments.*

When to give notes

In some contracts there are provisions where the actors cannot receive notes after *half hour*. This came from the days when directors would go into the actor's dressing room right up until the show, offering suggested changes. It was very stressful for the actor, so the rule was created to allow for the actor to focus on his/her show. As of *half-hour* the actor could be confident there would be no more changes made and could practise any recent changes from the rehearsal earlier that day.

There is no such rule in the Production Contract on Broadway. However, it is a courtesy not to give a bunch of notes between the *half-hour* call and the *places* call. There are some actors who do not even get to the theatre until *half-hour,* so it would be impossible to give notes to them following that rule. This is a personal preference for actors.

It's best to come early and give out notes to the actors who are there before *half hour*. You can find those actors who come in at *half hour* and give them notes as soon as they arrive. If there are still notes to give out to the performers, then you could say "I have a couple quick notes to give you. Do you want them now, or is there a better time?" They will likely say you can give them now. They would have the opportunity to say they need to eat or shower quickly, and it would be better after that. You will find that you don't always get your notes out to everyone. That is okay. It can wait another day. If there are notes that cannot wait, then put those at the top of your priority list to give out first.

Another option for giving notes is leaving a note card (index card) on the actor's dressing table. Some actors are fine with this, some may not be. You can always ask if an actor is fine with it. That way, you can write the note on a card, and they will get it before the show. If they don't understand, they will find you to ask a question. It saves time and running around.

Generally, you never give notes during intermission or after a show. There may be some actors who approach you during those times and ask you questions. You can answer those questions and give notes that pertain to their question if it seems appropriate. Do not actively go around the theatre and give notes during those times.

An exception would be an emergency or a planned rehearsal. An actor may get injured during a show and ask to do a lift a different way. You would have to find a moment to communicate with the other actor and give him/her that note. There may be pre-planned things to do during intermission if the actor has requested that time to rehearse. An example would be rehearsing a lift at intermission. Both actors could be given a note before the show and asked when it would be a good time to rehearse. If they suggest intermission, then you arrange to do it then.

> *TIP:*
> *It's a good idea to consult with the stage manager and let him/her know about any rehearsals at intermission. He/she is in charge of the crew and the crew has duties during intermission. (They might have to change over the set during intermission). The stage manager will want to make sure the crew is not inconvenienced and the actors are safe.*

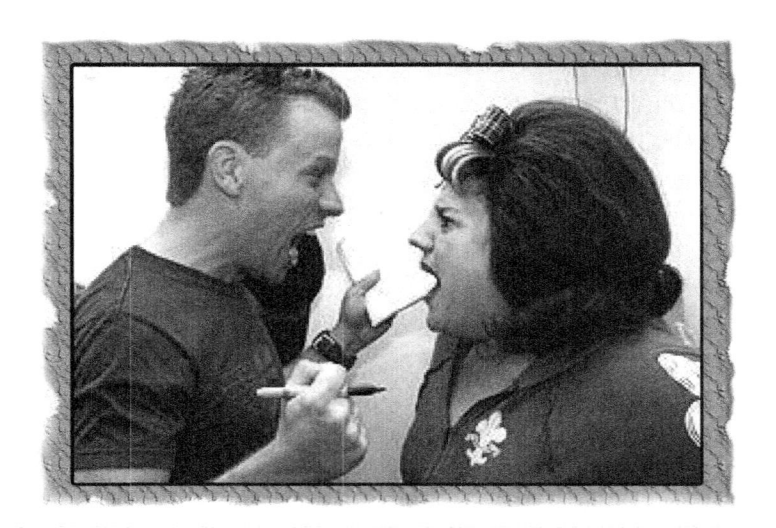

Dance captain "JUST TAKE THE NOTE!
Actress "I WON THE TONY!"
Dance captain "F%k!"*

Photo credit: Bruce Glikas
The above (completely exaggerated and staged) photo is Rusty Mowery, dance captain of Hairspray, and Marissa Jaret Winokur who played the lead "Tracy Turnblad".

Ways to give notes

There are a few ways to give notes to actors for a show:
1. Writing or typing everyone's notes on the callboard so the actors read it when they come in the door
2. Speaking face to face
3. Leaving note cards on their dressing room table
4. Making an announcement

You may see some directors post their company notes on the callboard. The actors will see the notes as they sign in for the show. This is something that should be used sparingly and not used for personal notes. It's okay to put some general notes for the full company on the board, such as "There is a lot of noise on stage left during the opening, and it's becoming audible in the house". At no time should you print up all your individual notes and post them on the callboard. No one wants other actors to read their mistakes, and no actor wants to waste time reading other actor's notes.

The best way to give notes and create relationships is face to face. This means approaching individual dressing rooms to give your notes in person. That way, the actor also has the opportunity to ask questions or communicate other problems he/she may have that cause issue. In old theatres, you will find many dressing rooms on multiple levels. You have to go up and down the stairs many times to give out notes before a show. You can always check the sign-in sheet on the callboard to see if an actor is in the building or not. Over time, the actors will likely have a pattern as to when they arrive each day. You will learn and find a pattern for each actor to give notes to and when.

If you are running out of time, you can write the note on a card and leave it on their dressing table. Some actors may prefer this as a regular solution too. You can ask the individual actors how and when they want to receive notes.

Finally, you can make an announcement over the speakers from the stage management office. It is not something you want to do often! Once in a while it's okay, if it's a general note for the whole company. If you do it sparingly, then actors will pay attention. If you use this method, make it short and clear.

"We had a swing, fresh out of college, for his Broadway debut who never really spoke up or reached out to anyone to get help on being a swing. The dance captain never once asked the swing if he needed anything or helped him. It became apparent in rehearsals that he was unprepared to go onstage. When the dance captain found out how much help he still needed, he chose to belittle him in front of everyone rather than help prepare him. It was embarrassing for the swing and really shook his confidence. The swing never got constructive encouragement, advice or guidance from our dance captain. The dance captain's attitude was basically 'tough luck' and it was a huge disservice to the swing, the rest of the cast, the crew and the show "
- Anonymous swing

"We had an onstage dance captain who never wrote a thing down to make a show bible, which would have helped us reference for accuracy. Then one day she approached one of swings in the dressing room to see if she could photocopy her notes! It wasn't to just get some help with creating her bible, it was to just blatantly copy the work of another hard-working swing and use it for teaching purposes. The dance captain came across as lazy and lost a lot of respect from the company for doing that."
- Anonymous swing

CHAPTER 9

Making a Show Bible

What is a show bible?

A show bible is a "book" that contains all the valuable information regarding a Broadway production. Each department makes their own bible containing needed information. A dance captain would make a bible to retain the multitude of things you need to know. It contains charts for every number showing where each actor is at any given moment. It can have staging charts, traffic patterns, choreography, pictures, clean up notes, and individual tracking sheets for each actor.

Nowhere does it say that you *have* to make a show bible. Each dance captain works differently and there are a few that don't use a bible. However, if you do not, you have to rely on your memory for every little detail. I have never met a dance captain who could retain all the show's details in his/her head.

A bible can be electronic or hard copy. A hard copy would likely be a large binder, 4-5" thick, with all the information on paper. An electronic bible is created on a computer. There is an ipad program called *Stage Write* specifically designed to make Broadway show bibles. We will get into more detail about *Stage Write* later in this chapter. This chapter will provide you with a number of ways to make a bible and what is most helpful to include.

Here's an example of a bible done on paper in a binder:

Here's an example of the same bible done electronically:

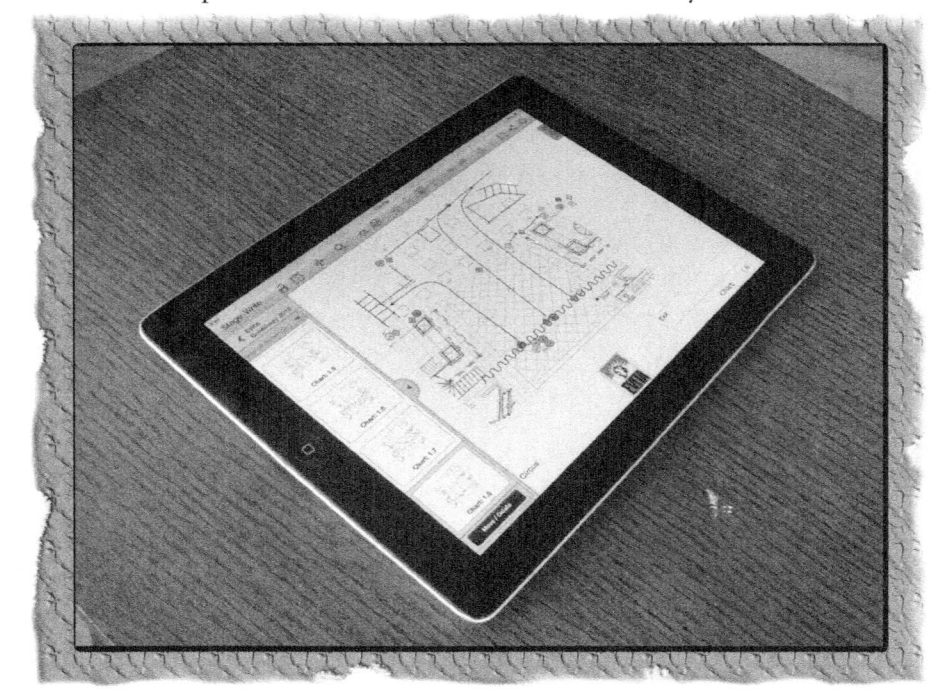

There are exceptional benefits to making a show bible.
1. You have access to an enormous amount of information without memorizing it.
2. It is a resource for others when you are absent.
3. The company respects a dance captain who has accurate information and it helps them to see the information on paper.
4. It's a good resource for swings and understudies.
5. It's a guide for the next dance captain if you leave a show.
6. It's a valuable resource when a tour is mounted and you are asked to be a part of the mounting team.

What to include in the bible

Here are some suggestions what to include to facilitate your job as a dance captain:
1. Staging charts (more commonly referred to as just *charts*)
2. Staging notes
3. Choreography
4. Tracking sheets for each actor
5. Other helpful information pertinent to the show

Charts

Staging is different from choreography. Choreography is the movement you learn. Staging is where you are placed on stage while doing the choreography. Charts are "overhead snapshots" of the stage, showing where each actor is placed at any given time during the show. To keep track of where the actors are on stage, you need a detailed recording system. This will be a personal preference. This chapter will give you some suggestions. There could be a few hundred charts in a show, depending on how long a show is and how intricate each number is.

If you are starting a new show, ask the stage manager, on the first rehearsal day for a table at the front of the room. You need an easily accessible, consistent place to put your things. You will want to write as much information as quickly as the choreographer gives it. You may also want to have a clipboard so you have a place to put the charts from the number you are working on. This way you can walk around the room freely, making sure you get accurate information.

Here's are two examples of a chart:

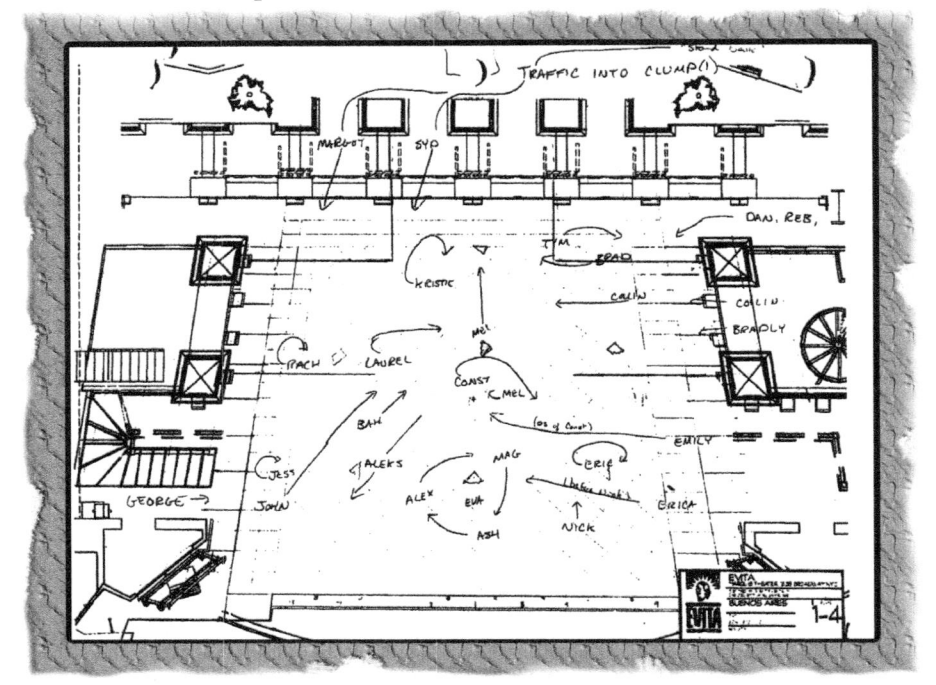

The chart below is the same stage position, done electronically:

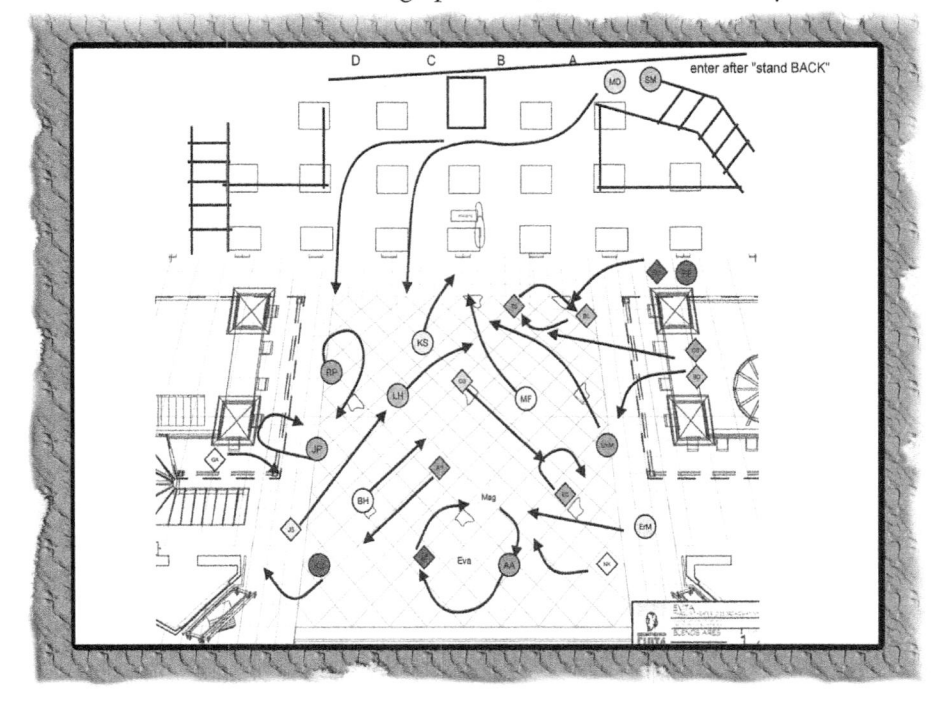

There will likely be some form of measurement used when staging each number. Some shows will have numbers at the front of the stage. This helps position the actors "**width-wise**" from left to right on the entire stage. When using numbers, the center mark is zero and the measurement gets larger on each side, stage left and stage right. You may be told, "move stage right to 5" or, "put your left foot on stage left 12". That would mean move 5 feet stage right of center or 12 feet stage left of center.

Some shows choose to have colored lights across the front instead of numbers. You may be told, "go between the blue and yellow" or "stand on green". It can get very specific, especially when you are working with large casts and creating detailed, balanced pictures with the choreographer.

Most importantly, the stage is two dimensional. The choreographer and director may also tell actors where to be "**depth-wise**". They may use the wings, marks on the stage or *tracks* where automation will run. This helps with the placement of actors depth-wise from upstage to downstage. For accuracy, you have to mark where the actors are, both left to right and upstage to downstage. You may have to walk around the room while actors are being positioned, so you can see exactly where they are placed in relationship to other actors.

> *TIP:*
> *What to do if there are no numbers...*
>
> *Take a look at the stage and write down any markings that are consistent throughout the show that can be used as reference. (tracks, wings, speakers, set pieces, platforms)*

Here are some different ways to make charts:

1. Write *many* stage positions on one (lined) page.
2. Write *many* stage positions on one (blank) page.
3. Write *one* stage position per page using the production stage charts.
4. Write *one* stage position per page using blank paper.
5. Input everything into Stage Write, the ipad app.

Once the choreographer starts to stage, get the overall information down in one large book. Grab a sharp pencil, a good eraser and lots of paper or your ipad. The paper can be lined, blank or stage graphs of the scene you are working on.

Include any special direction the choreographer or director say. It could be numbers they want actors to be on, props they hold, intentions, words to move on, or anything else they deem important.

1. **Here's an example of using lined paper**: (The "built-in" lines are helpful for placing actors in the same line for any production number.)

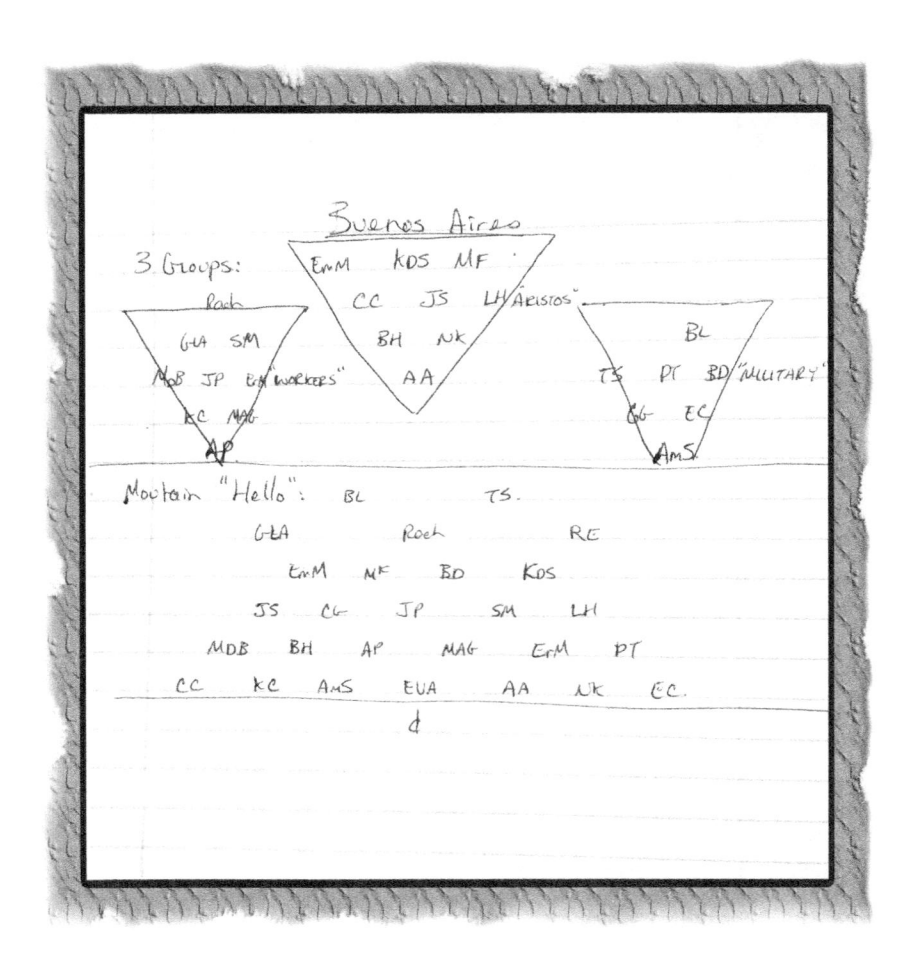

- Making a Show Bible -

2. **Here's an example of using a blank piece of paper:** (It's great because it gives you lots of room for notes. You may have to write in more information than you would if you used blank stage graphs.)

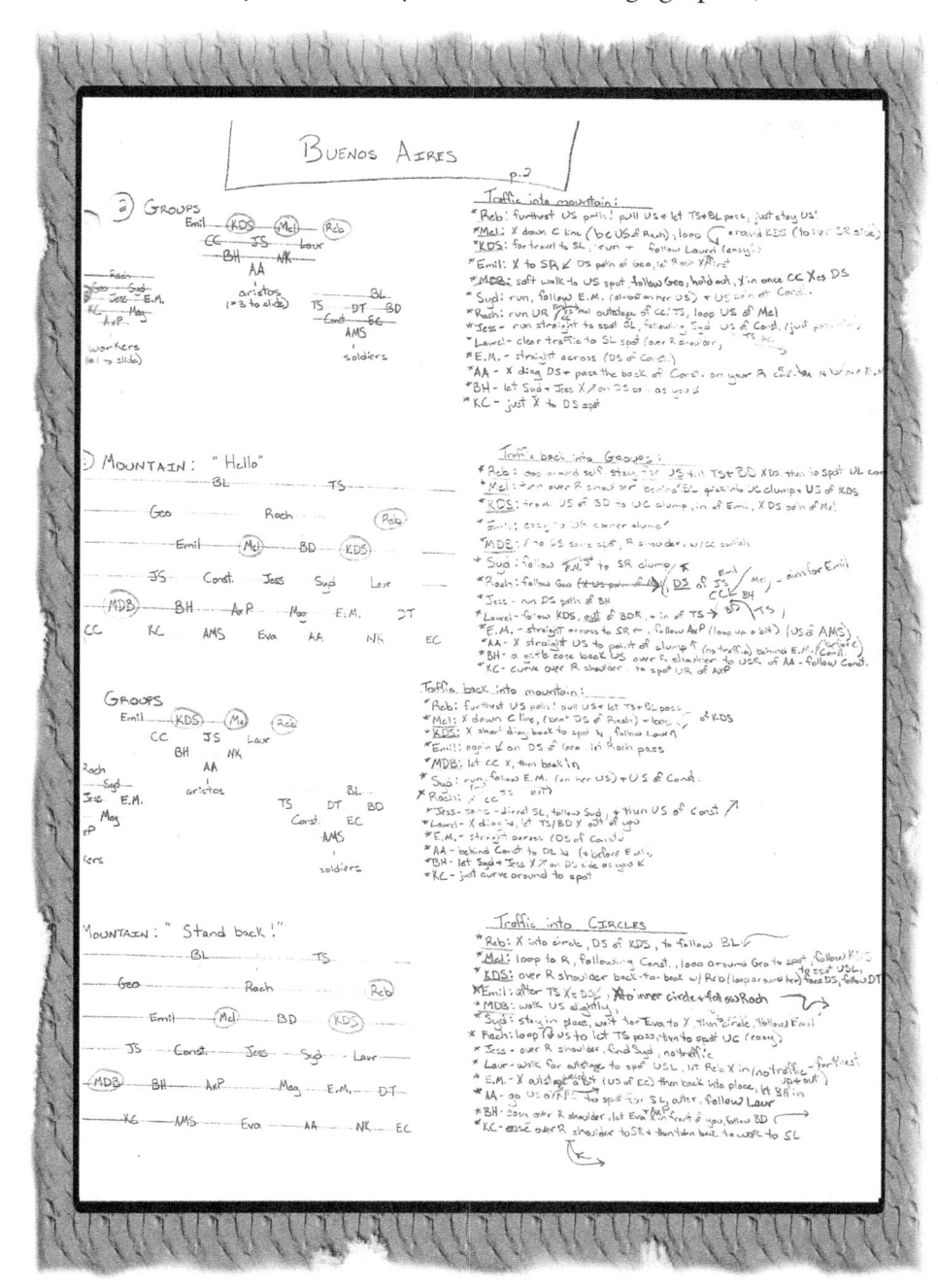

[Handwritten staging notes page titled "Buenos Aires p.2", showing group formations and traffic patterns for a musical number. The page includes diagrams of stage positions for characters (Reb, Mel, KDS, Emil, MDB, Sud, Rach, Jess, Laur, E.M., AA, BH, KC, etc.) in three configurations labeled "Groups," "Mountain: 'Hello'," and "Mountain: 'Stand back!'," with detailed traffic/blocking notes for transitions between each formation on the right side of the page.]

The strength of the previous example is that it is easy to look at all the diagrams quickly with lots of information on one page. The downside is you would have to write in all the information, such as numbers and tracks and such. You can leave information out to keep it looking cleaner, but your note-taking will be less specific.

3. **Here's an example using a production stage chart**: (It is useful to quickly chart where an actor goes. You can see the numbers, tracks, and wings.) The "production" stage chart just means this was created by the set designer for the show and is exactly what you will see onstage.

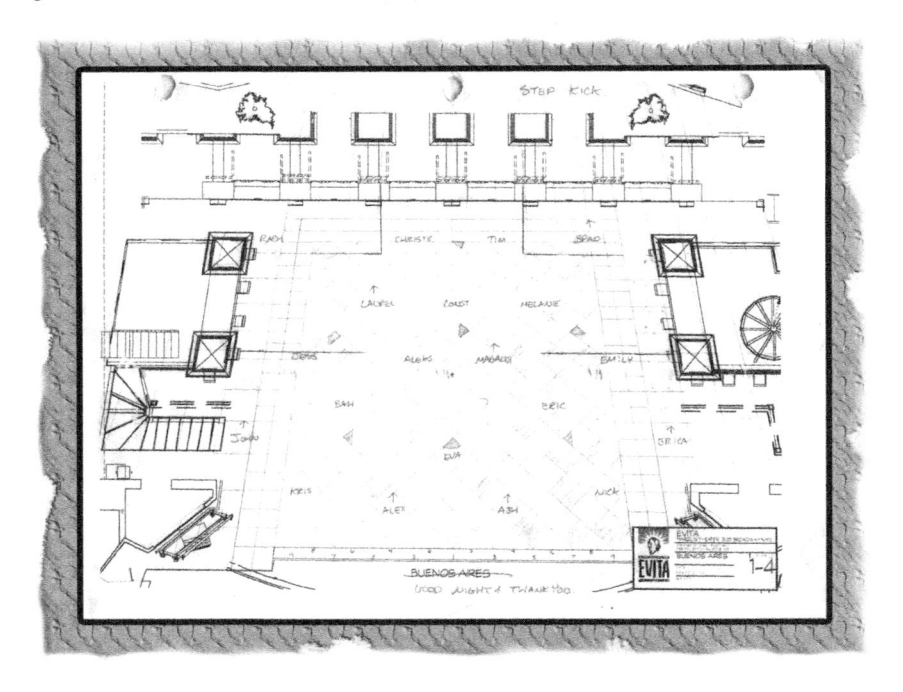

As the director or choreographer is placing the actors, write down their location on the chart. You will have a new chart for every major position change throughout the number. It is helpful to title each chart using lyrics, dialogue, or specific references (such as "the clump" or "the mountain"). You will have numerous charts for one number. It's important to keep your system labeled and organized.

You can ask stage management if they have any blank production stage charts. It is commonly called a *chart*. There are different charts for every scene. They can be photocopied to any size, but you would probably start with a regular 8 1/2" x 11" piece of paper.

Here is an example of a blank production stage chart:

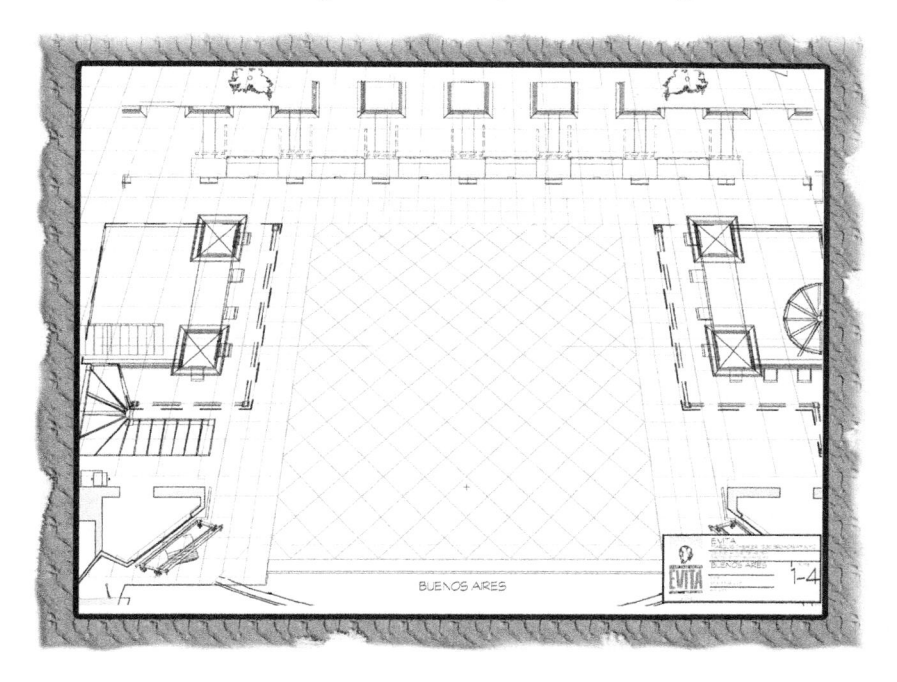

If there are no charts created, the stage manager may ask the set designer for a template. A production assistant (PA) may be asked to make copies. It's not part of their job, so be gracious and very appreciative.

> *TIP:*
> *It's a good idea to number your pages if you decide to use paper. If you happen to drop them and they scatter, you want the ability to put them in order quickly for immediate reference.*

> *TIP:*
> *Don't get rid of ANY charts until you have finalized your permanent bible! There will be numerous notes you have to transfer and there are times when the creative team will want to go back to an old version they did.*

Instead of writing people's names on the chart, you can create a shorthand for identifying who they are. You could use their initials or character names. If you don't know their last names, then write their full first names or whatever you can to get started. Using character names is always helpful, especially when an actor is replaced by another. You won't have to change the names in your charts.

Here's an example of the **chart filled in with initials** instead of names.

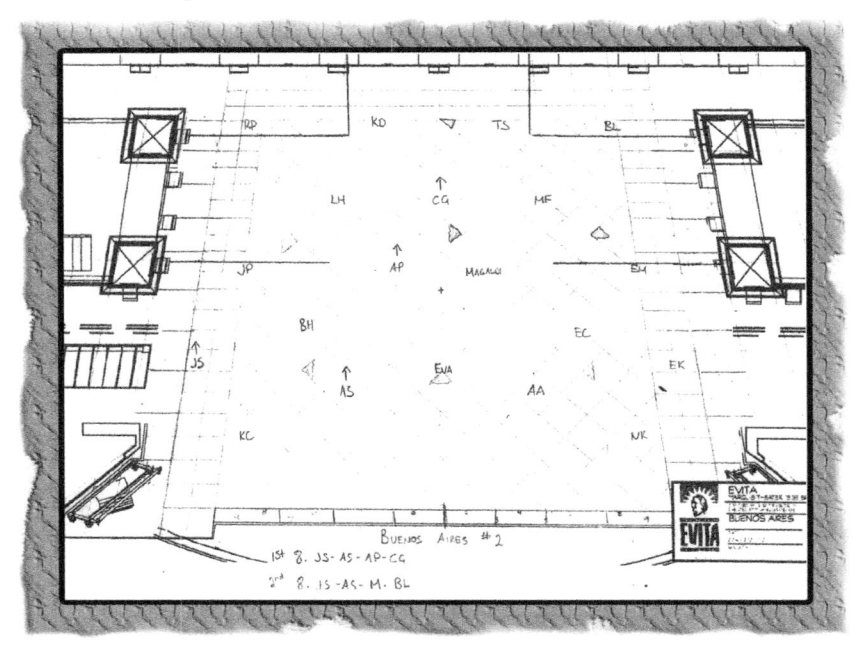

Ultimately your first pass will be "draft charts", and you can perfect your system later. It will go quickly, and it will be messy. The most important thing is to write down *everything* you can. There will be many changes, so write in pencil!

> *TIP:*
> *It's a good idea to place your papers on a clipboard and have a pencil and eraser close so you have freedom to walk around the room while jotting down spacing. (Attach the pencil to the clipboard with velcro or magnetized tape)*

4. Write one stage position per page using blank paper:

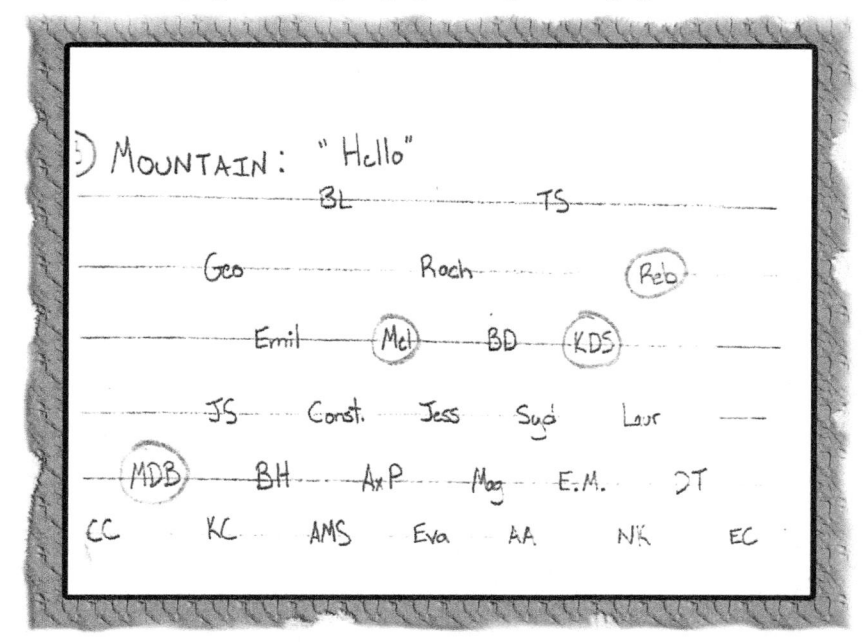

> MOUNTAIN: "Hello"
> BL   TS
>   Geo   Rach   (Reb)
>   Emil—(Mel)—BD—(KDS)
>   JS   Const.   Jess   Sud   Lor
>   (MDB)   BH   AxP   Mog   E.M.   DT
>   CC   KC   AMS   Eva   AA   NK   EC

    In this instance, the dance captain places the positions on a blank piece of paper. Lines are drawn to show the actors who should be in the same line. There is a title showing what position it relates to in the music. The only things missing are the numbers but the position is very clear and easy to read.

5. Stage Write application:

    There is a new application for the ipad called Stage Write. It allows you to upload blank stage charts (jpeg format) to create your bible. It has many helpful features. The pros of this program are that it doesn't waste paper. You can save many versions, you switch between audience and performer point of views and it's easy to email or print. If the stage manager calls to tell you too many people are out and you have to create a *split-track*, you are more likely to have your ipad with you than your bulky dance captain bible. The con is your ipad relies on battery power. You always want the information accessible. You could make an electronic version and print it or email it to have a second copy. It takes practise to become quick using the program, but it is nice to walk around with a simple ipad. To learn more about this app, visit www.stagewritesoftware.com or check out tutorials on You Tube.

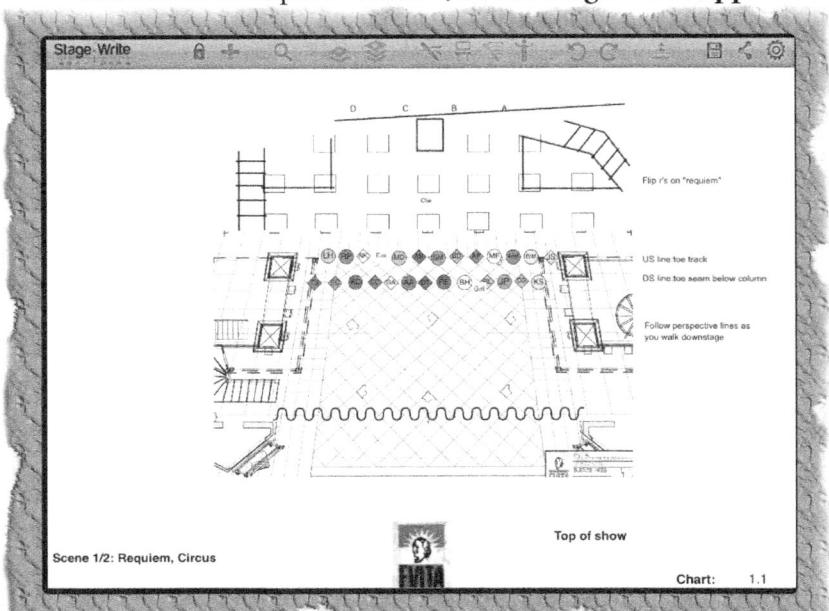

Here is an example of a **chart, in the Stage Write app**.

Do you prefer the Audience or Actor's point of view?

Here's an example of an alternate version, from an actor's point of view.

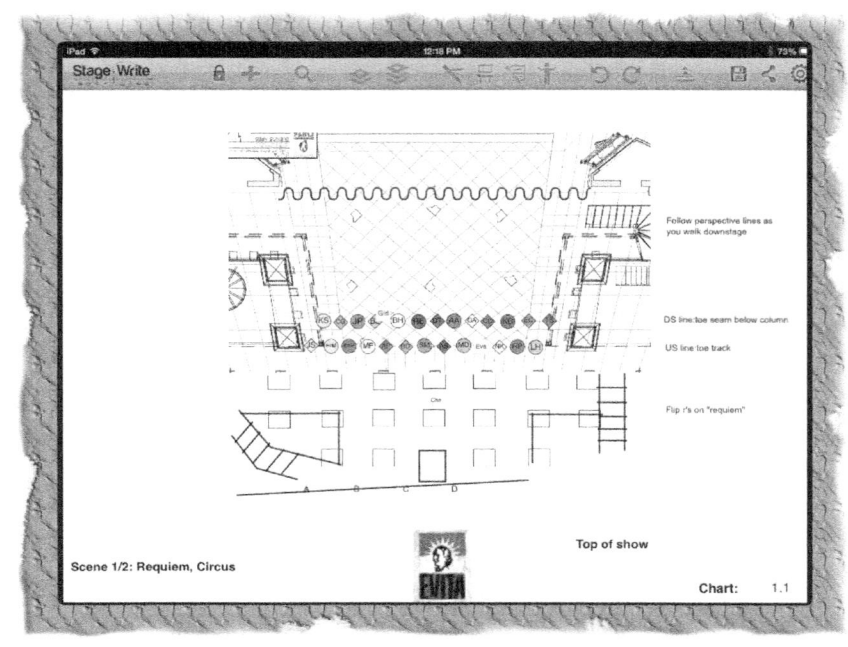

Write everything down

Extensive writing is what will make you stand out in the long run. You can't possibly keep all things in your head, so write everything down. It be useful later and will give you "street credibility" when you state what the director's intentions were a month from now. If you are a swing, you have an advantage here so make the most of it! The rest of the cast is on their feet so they do not have the luxury of carrying a pencil and paper. They may forget the details down the road.

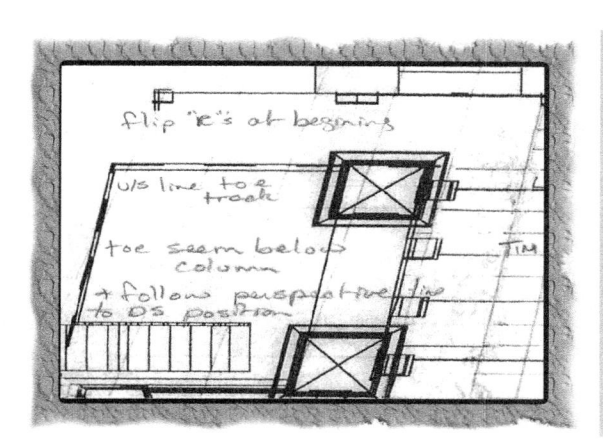

Write everything you hear in the corner of your chart that pertains to that number.

The musical director asked everyone to flip their "R's" singing Requiem.

The choreographer placed the two lines specifically for lighting (toe track and toe seam below column).

The director wanted the actors to walk downstage following the perspective lines on the stage vs walking straight downstage.

When writing the information down for the first time, you can sit or walk around as the company is being placed. You could sit at the swing table or at your own space you created somewhere in the rehearsal room. If you walk around, it's best to have a clipboard to put your papers on so you have a "mobile table" to write on.

TIP:
Have you ever played the telephone game? You whisper what you heard from the person on one side of you to the person on the other side of you. The final person "repeats" what the first person said. It's rarely correct! The moral of the story is to write down the specifics because you will NEVER remember the exact words and intentions given. Those details are golden!

Once the show is near opening, the show gets *frozen*. A show is *frozen* when no more changes are made. That's when you can make a *permanent* bible. It's best to wait until the show is frozen to eliminate unnecessary work, to keep your notes up to date and accurate. The attention to detail in your final bible is going to separate you from being a good dance captain to being an extraordinary one! This becomes your "life-line" of answers. The more specific you are, the better. No brain can handle all the details of an entire show for every actor!

Here's an example of a "first draft" chart: (It was done before getting on stage, so the positions are vague compared to the final version.)

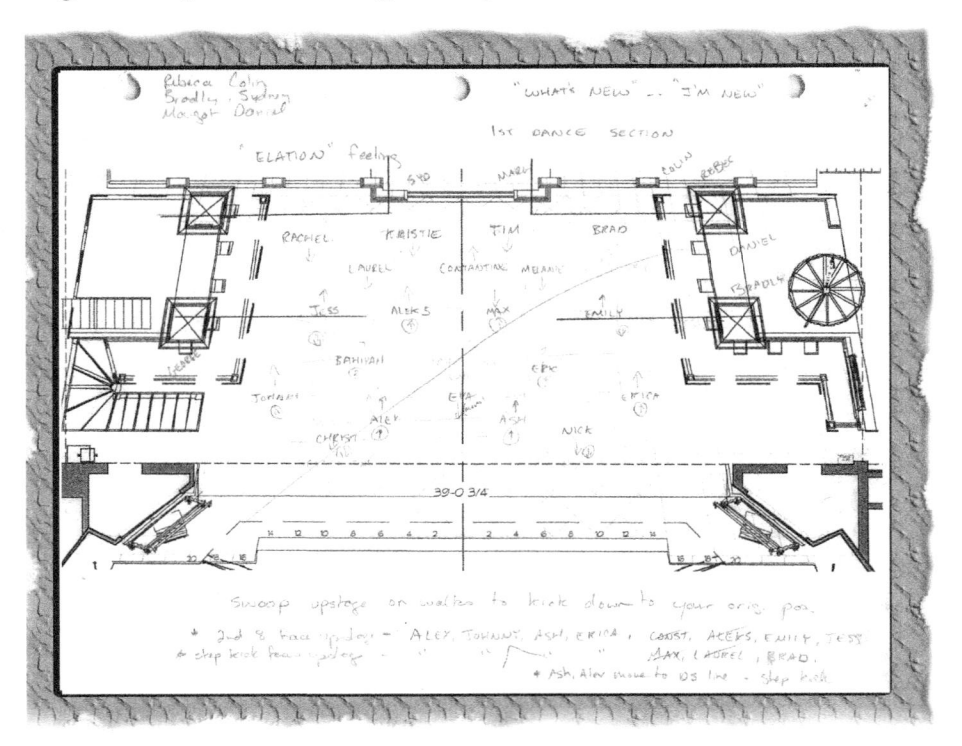

You will find major changes between your first and your permanent charts. There are many changes once you get to the actual stage. There may be more markings you can use as references, such as wings or tracks you didn't have before.

In the case of *EVITA*, there were no numbers on the stage. Once the cast was onstage, there were "diamond" markings and speakers on the stage floor that helped with specifically placing the actors.

Here's an example of a "permanent" chart (of the same stage position):

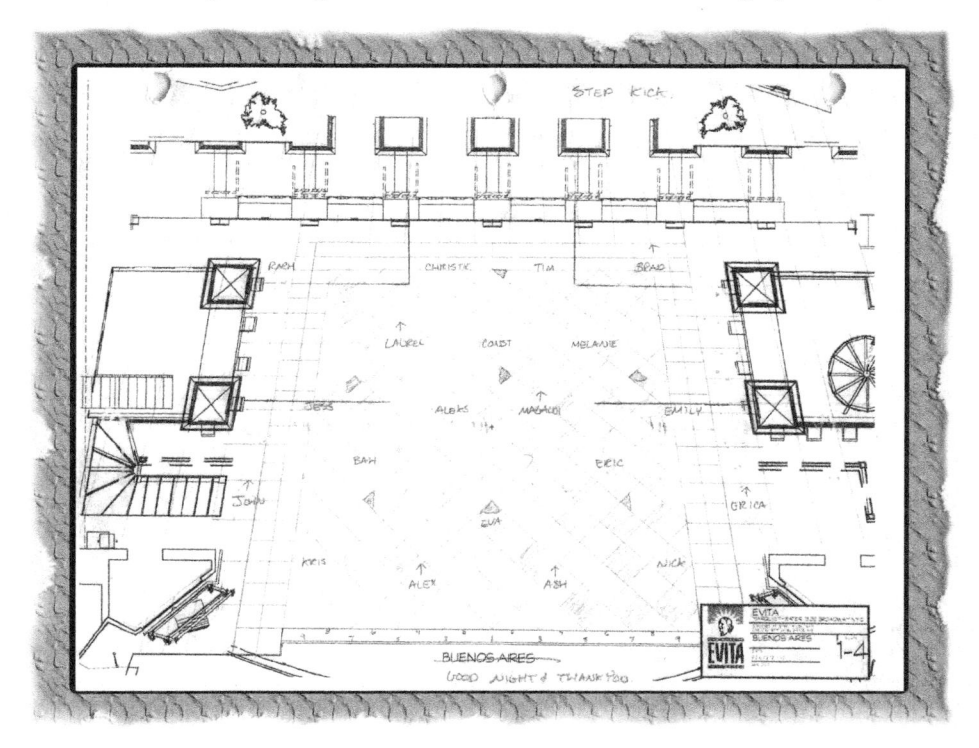

Once you get on stage, you may find the front edge of the stage has a 6 foot drop to the audience's seats. Many actors are not comfortable standing close to the edge, even though they were blocked there in the studio. Many of these elements change when you move from the studio to the stage, but your notes will ultimately help you with your specificity and details.

These charts are written from the perspective of the audience because that is where the dance captain learned the positions. She also watched the show from this point of view, so she chose to write like this. You can also switch the graphs 180 degrees and write it from the actor's point of view. There is no right or wrong way and there are benefits to both. It depends on how you process information.

> *TIP:*
> *When you are finished getting all the information off an old chart, just strike a line through it so you know it's an old chart. This will help keep you organized and minimize confusion regarding which chart to look at!*

Messy to Marvelous

    No matter what your method is, expect it will go through a process to get it to where you want. The final product will look marvelous, but the originals will seem messy. Don't get too hung up on the look in the beginning. Concentrate on gathering as much information as you can, quickly. The show bible will have copious information to gather for various sections; charts, staging notes, tracks sheets and so forth.

    On the following page you will see an example of a temporary, first draft chart versus the permanent, final chart below it. The original chart contains much detailed information that the final chart does not. This original chart is from EVITA. It was the moment after Juan Peron is elected and everyone had gathered to see and cheer him on. It was the moment before Eva's famous song on the balcony "Don't cry for me Argentina". The original chart has everything written from what the director said, to who is holding hankies. Some important information from this chart is:

- The director told the cast they are seeing the "newly elected" Juan Peron, for the first time.
- It was choreographed so the curtain would go up while everyone cheered and spread out, to fill the stage once the curtain flew out.
- The cast was told to bring their vocal shouts down when Che started to speak.
- The cast was told to make their bodies face directly upstage, yet take their focus to the center of the balcony. This made the stage look more full than if everyone's bodies were facing towards center.
- The cast was facing upstage away from the conductor and couldn't see the monitor. Johnny was the onstage conductor for cut off's.
- Everyone was told to shake their hankies when they sang the last "Evita" and stop shaking when the music stopped.
- Everyone had to bring two hankies onstage (They used one and hid one) except for the maids, who exited during the number. When the maids exited, everyone would wave their second hanky to make it look like there were still the same number of people onstage.

    You can put this information in the "staging notes" part of your bible so the final chart is not so "crowded". Then draw a line through the original chart so you know it's not the most recent one you are referencing.

- Making a Show Bible -

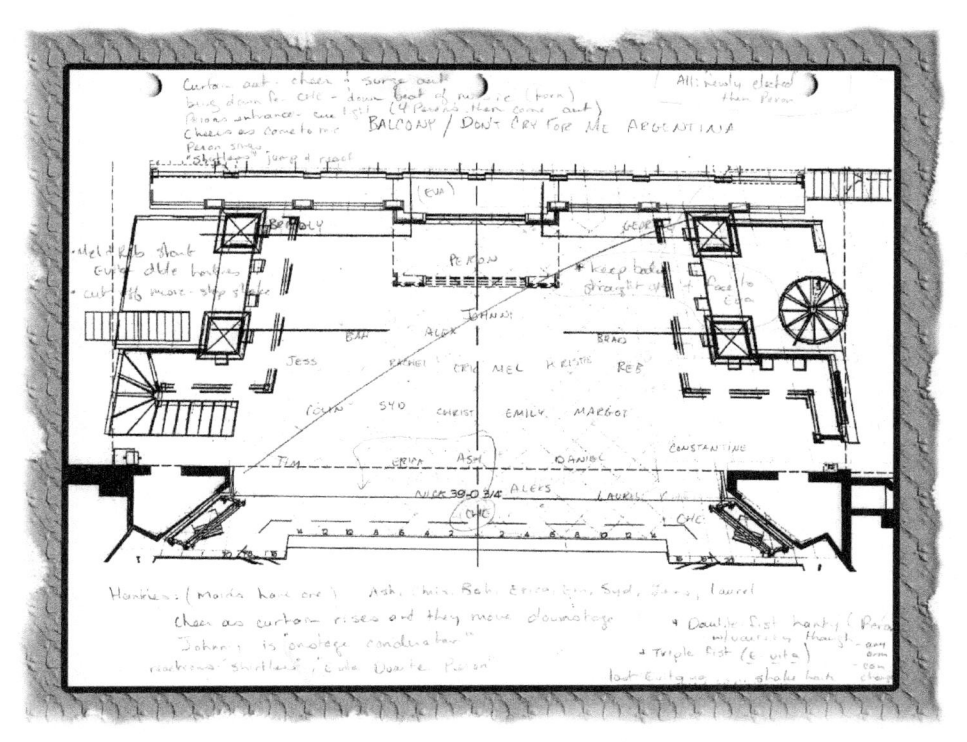

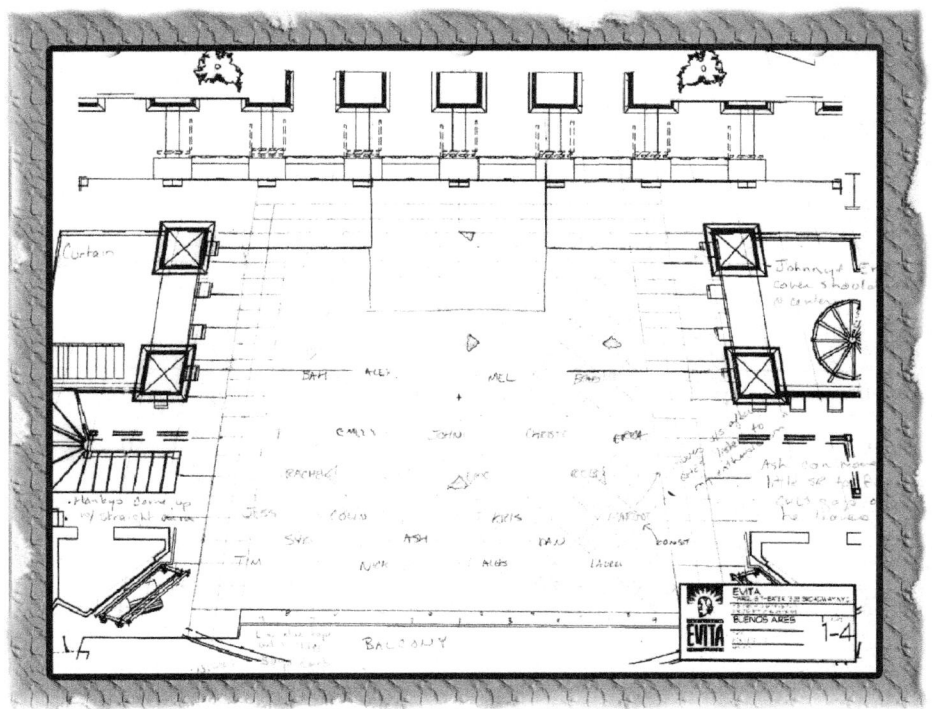

Staging Notes

Staging is where the actors are placed on the stage at any given moment during the show. Aside from charting, there is an additional way to detail information so it's easy to read and quickly accessible.

Here's an example of *staging notes*:

MONEY 09.08.12
(Guy's Choreography for Dance Break)

1-3 1-3		GUYS: "Water" step to L (1) to SL, end with R foot behind (3), Step RL (12) to SR, flick kick R (3)
1-3 1-3		GUYS: "Water" step facing upstage L (1) to SR, end R foot behind and face front (3), ball change back R (1), LR (23)
1-3 1-3		GUYS: Jump up (1) off R foot with L leg out to 90 degrees (arms up) then envelope in and land on R and present arms to her R over L (3). Lift the girl off the ground and tilt arms to SL for her fan (3)
1-3 1-3		GUYS: Step R (1) to SL, drag L (2) turning to R while still holding girl's R hand, step L foot together (3). Ball change back R (1), step L (2) and grab girl for sit lift. R hand around her R knee and inner thigh. L hand under and around butt. She will bring her L leg up to other.
1-3 1-3		GUYS: Lift girl and turn her to your left (CCW)..123, put her down SL of you 123. (2 turns)
1-3 1-3 1-3	*(Thank God for Switzerland music)*	GUYS: Spin to the left with arms out and head up. Do as many rotations as you can with feet out of time to music.
1-3 1-3		GUYS: Step out LRL (123) to SL (turning to the left) arms out-up-out and head to SL, "Water" Step R drag L (facing front) with arms free and moving up body with head free and moving up.
1-3 1-3		GUYS: Step out LRL (&123) facing upstage this time and use catch step (ball change) to get into it. Face front and do ball change back R(1), LR (23)
1-3 1-3		GUYS: Forward roll (L shoulder to R hip) (12), then stand up on L foot and pivot U/S to face girl (3). Step LRL (to meet girl) and let her fan kick (3) while you face U/S
1-3 1-3		GUYS: Step LR (12), fan kick L (3) facing the front. Step L plant R (12) to spin around and face the front and dip girl (3)
1-3 1-3		GUYS: Bring the girl up (1), step out L (2) to SL, bring R foot into L (2) with arms up, step out L (3) to SL with arms out. Step out L (1) to SL and arms out, bring R foot to L (2) while grabbing girls torso with L arm and bringing her to you. Step out lunge L (3) to SL while grabbing girl's L hamstring above her knee.
1-3		GUYS: Bring girl up onto her leg (1), step L (2) while switching arm grip, step out lunge R (3) while grabbing girl's R ankle.

The document was created on Microsoft Word:
- Select a new "blank document"
- Write the name of the show and the number on the top of the page
- You can add the date as well, to keep yourself more organized
- Insert table (3 columns and 20 rows to start out a document)
- Then you can adjust what you want inside the document (width of columns, size and style of font, centering, etc)

It helps to make a table with information such as:
1. Counts of the music (first column on the left)
2. Lyrics and script (second column)
3. Which actors are involved in the moment (right column)
4. What the actors are doing at the moment (right column)
5. Reference to what choreography actors are doing at that time (right column)

This system helps you in understudy rehearsal when you have to teach multiple people at the same time. It's nice to quickly access a document that tells you what all the actors are doing at the same time. Similarly, you can separate out each actor, if you are teaching just one person. You can save a copy of your document and delete any information you don't need. Then you retitle and resave your new document that is just for one or two actors, whoever you are rehearsing with.

> *TIP:*
> *To be prepared during rehearsals, you can create a table with just lyrics (and perhaps counts) and leave ample space in the third column to fill in (with pencil) while you learn the information. Then you can computerize it later.*

Even once you get a "permanent bible", be open to change. There are times when *brush up rehearsals* happen and minor things change that were perhaps missed in the haste of getting the show up. Traffic may be altered to help make it easier, and it could change whether an actor goes upstage or downstage of someone else. There will be things you learn and add along the way. An actor might find they would benefit from changing the way they did something before, and you will need to change it in your bible.

In the following staging notes, you can get a good idea of what everyone is doing on the stage at the same time. This one page has the details of about 10 charts. The staging notes and the charts work well together. Depending on what information you need, you can retrieve it quickly. If you need to see a stage formation quickly, you would look at the chart. If you need to see what PERON does to start the number, then you can look at the staging notes.

EVITA

09.08.12

Broadway Revival 2012

Art of the Possible

	Music from lovers	
	Drum roll	Peron: enters from SR and walks to center and faces front. (Start R foot, walk 11 steps, stop, turn, stamp R foot) TIM: walks on the balcony from SL and gets to Center at the same time Peron does.
1-6		Men: start walking DS on R foot immediately.
1-6		
1-3		
1-3	*Men: One has no rules. Is not precise.*	"Precise" all step RLR.
1-6		
1-6	*One rarely acts the same way twice.*	"Twice" all step LRL
1-6		
1-6	*(*) One spurns no Device.*	MEN: walk in a circle R foot before singing.
1-6		
1-8	*Practising the art of the*	Walk into circle L foot. PERON: is USR in circle.
1-6	*Possible.*	PERON: ends up USR DAN/CONSTANTINE: "possible" (12), step x R in front (3), step L(5)
1-6		Continue slow steps R(1), L(3), R(5) while the arms slowly come up and lock.
1-6		Grapevine L(1), step R behind (2), step L (3), R in front (4), L(5), point R leg back (6)
1-6		Ronde jamb (123), DAN lifts foot (45), leg down (61)
1-4		DAN lands his leg (1), and flicks to hook (2)
1-6		They struggle and Dan steps to SR facing upstage and throws Constantine to the floor SL with his head facing DS
	One always picks the easy fight.	MEN: Sing then start pacing on the upstage leg "Always". Pivot, step, together "fight" PERON and Bradley cross to SL (US of Brad) CONSTANTINE: get up and go DSR for a moment then cross upstage. DAN: stands at center facing front.
	One praises fools. One smothers light.	MEN: continue to walk on upstage foot "praises". Pivot, step together "light". The all men start on R foot to walk in circle (56) before singing.
	(*) One shifts left to right.	MEN: continue to walk in circle L,R,L,R,L,R

Choreography

When learning choreography, take comfortable clothes and shoes to dance in. You should also take a pencil, eraser and some paper to write on. The paper depends on your personal preference: loose leaf, blank, lined, coiled notebook, binder. A clipboard can come in handy when you need to walk around the room and jot things down.

If the choreographer starts by teaching general dance terminology on "its feet", then grab an area of the dance floor and learn along with the rest of the company. If it looks like the choreographer will be spacing the number while teaching the choreography, then it's best to have your personal system of notation ready to write everything down.

Don't worry about writing the choreography down immediately as you are learning it. It's best to get it into your body first. You can write it down on a break or after you learn it that day. You will need to refer to it later. Not even Superman would be able to remember the little choreography nuances you will learn. By the time you have learned many people's choreography and nuances, you will be glad you wrote the details down.

There are many ways to help remember:

1. Write the choreography in your score next to the corresponding music.
2. Write the choreography on a blank piece of paper.
3. Tape yourself doing the choreography.

1. Here's an example of writing the choreography in your score.

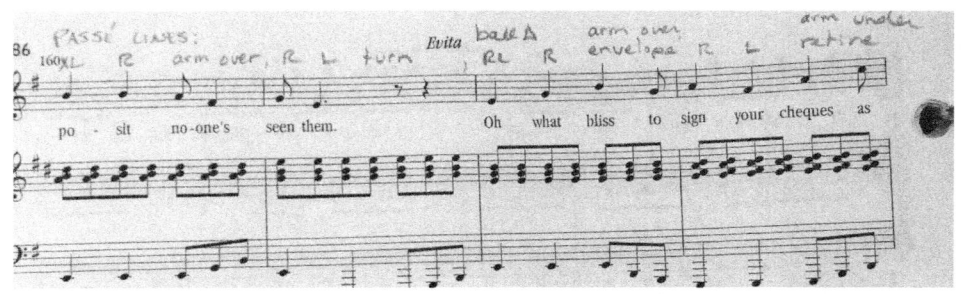

2. Here's an example of writing the choreography on a blank piece of paper.

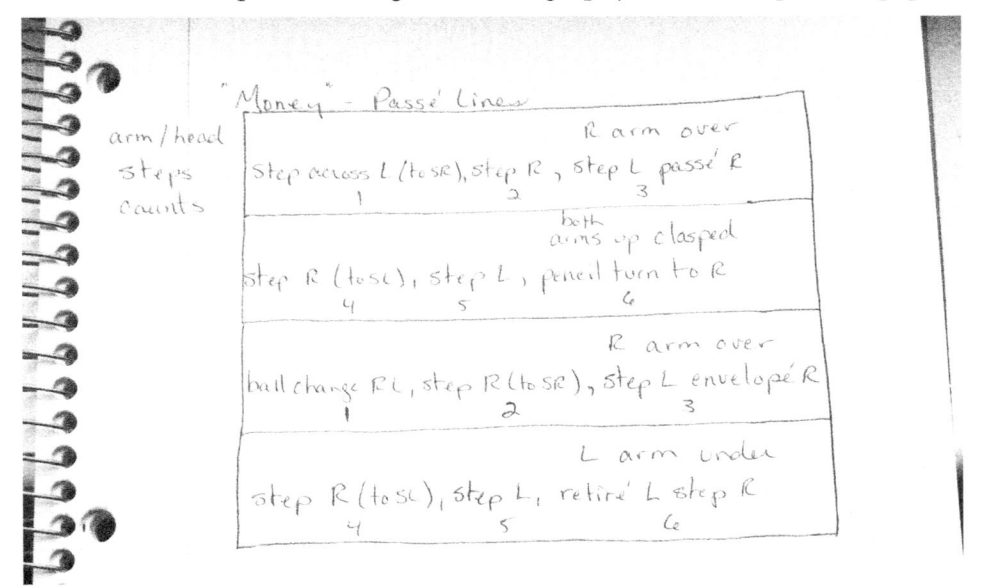

```
"Money" - Passé Lines

arm/head                              R arm over
steps     Step across L (to SR), step R, step L passé R
counts              1              2          3

                                      both
                                      arms up clasped
          step R (to SL), step L, pencil turn to R
                 4          5              6

                                      R arm over
          ball change RL, step R (to SR), step L envelope R
                1              2              3

                                      L arm under
          step R (to SL), step L, retiré L step R
                 4          5           6
```

3. You can also video tape yourself with a phone, video camera, ipad, computer, flip cam, and so forth. Remind yourself of specific notes, such as "remember your head is downstage on count 1". When you review it, you will have all the information you need. The more the better.

When writing down choreography, there are a number of components that you can include to be effective, helping yourself later.

You should include:
1. What is happening with the head and arms.
2. The particular actions of the body (particularly the feet).
3. The counts or timing of the dance steps.

TIP:
Avoid the possibility of insulting a choreographer by dancing someone else's choreography in front of him/her. I saw a dancer practising choreography from another show during a rehearsal break. The cast was enjoying it but our choreographer was very offended and reprimanded him. You never know what pressure and stress the choreographer is going through.

TIP:
Stick-figure drawings are useful to help you remember. They are most helpful when actors are given specific poses by the choreographer needed when you go on for their track.

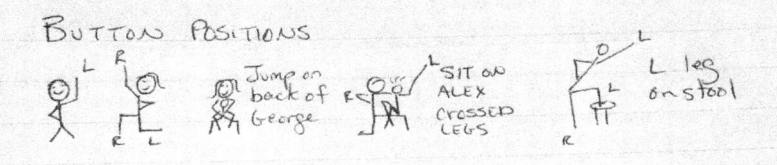

BUTTON POSITIONS

[handwritten stick-figure notes: "L R" pose; Jump on back of George; SIT ON ALEX CROSSED LEGS; L leg on stool]

TIP:
You may develop your own short hand notation to aid you in writing down choreography. In the example below, the dance captain chose to use a triangle symbol for every "ball change" instead of writing words each time. The "x" was used every time you were to cross one foot over the other.

△ L R = Ball change L R.

X L R = Cross L foot over R and step R.

Here is an example of the choreography quickly handwritten. It was later computerized with more detail, for a show bible. It doesn't need to be pretty; it needs to retain information you need later. You can tell the music is counted in 3's (123, 123). "Water" is a term that the choreographer used for a step he created.

Guys

1-3 Water to L, step RL flick kick R
1-3

1-3 step LR up (face fnt), back R, LR, jump
   face U/S   L leg out
                                         envelope
1-3   arms up
___

Left girl
drag L step R to + turn her, step bk R ball △
That's open arm — step in L RLR - - -

___

to SC LRL (turn to L, water drag ◯
to SR (facing U/S), ball △ back R, LR, roll
to girl RLR, LR kick L
step L plant R dip girl

___

girl up   , step out (3),

Here is an example of the choreography, cleaned up and clarified, for a show bible. It is more specific regarding what choreography is happening on each count of music. It was created using a table in Microsoft Word. The left column has the counts of the music. The second column contains the lyrics of the song. The third column has the choreography that relates to the music at that time.

MONEY
(Guy's Choreography for Dance Break)

Counts	Lyrics	Choreography
1-3 1-3		GUYS: "Water" step to L (1) to SL, end with R foot behind (3), Step RL (12) to SR, flick kick R (3)
1-3 1-3		GUYS: "Water" step facing upstage L (1) to SR, end R foot behind and face front (3), ball change back R (1), LR (23)
1-3 1-3		GUYS: Jump up (1) off R foot with L leg out to 90 degrees (arms up) then envelope in and land on R and present arms to her R over L (3). Lift the girl off the ground and tilt arms to SL for her fan (3)
1-3 1-3		GUYS: Step R (1) to SL, drag L (2) turning to R while still holding girl's R hand, step L foot together (3). Ball change back R (1), step L (2) and grab girl for sit lift. R hand around her R knee and inner thigh. L hand under and around butt. She will bring her L leg up to other.
1-3 1-3		GUYS: Lift girl and turn her to your left (CCW)..123, put her down SL of you 123. (2 turns)
1-3 1-3 1-3	*(Thank God for Switzerland music)*	GUYS: Spin to the left with arms out and head up. Do as many rotations as you can with feet out of time to music.
1-3 1-3		GUYS: Step out LRL (123) to SL (turning to the left) arms out-up-out and head to SL, "Water" Step R drag L (facing front) with arms free and moving up body with head free and moving up.
1-3 1-3		GUYS: Step out LRL (&123) facing upstage this time and use catch step (ball change) to get into it. Face front and do ball change back R(1), LR (23)
1-3 1-3		GUYS: Forward roll (L shoulder to R hip) (12), then stand up on L foot and pivot U/S to face girl (3). Step LRL (to meet girl) and let her fan kick (3) while you face U/S
1-3 1-3		GUYS: Step LR (12), fan kick L (3) facing the front. Step L plant R (12) to spin around and face the front and dip girl (3)
1-3 1-3		GUYS: Bring the girl up (1), step out L (2) to SL, bring R foot into L (2) with arms up, step out L (3) to SL with arms out. Step out L (1) to SL and arms out, bring R foot to L (2) while grabbing girls torso with L arm and bringing her to you. Step out lunge L (3) to SL while grabbing girl's L hamstring above her knee.
1-3		GUYS: Bring girl up onto her leg (1), step L (2) while switching arm grip, step out lunge R (3) while grabbing girl's R ankle.

Tracking Sheets for Each Actor

Now that you have the picture of the show "as a whole", you can break down the information in more detail for each actor. This will be helpful to have in your bible when you are teaching a track to an actor. If it's a new show, there will be numerous changes before opening night, so you might wait until the show is *frozen* to complete this part of your bible. This portion of the bible might be something you add to each time you teach a new track. Don't worry about getting all of the tracks down immediately. There is too much to do! Just do one at a time. It may even take a year to get all the tracking sheets done for the entire show if you decide to include them in your bible.

It helps to have individual tracking sheets so you can easily and efficiently teach a swing, an understudy or a replacement actor a track. It's difficult to sift through all the information for an entire show to obtain the specific information for one actor in rehearsal.

To start, make "rough" individual tracking sheets, as needed. These won't contain all the details of each track, but at least you can get by if you have to teach a swing or an understudy. It should include important information like props, entrances and exits, any dancing or singing features, partners, and so forth.

> *TIP:*
> *This is where the swings can become very valuable to you! The swings are usually assigned tracks to cover and each swing will have created a way of knowing an actor's role throughout the entire show. Perhaps they can share that information with you and save you time. Again, it's not their job to give this information, but it sure helps you. Be appreciative of the help!*

Here's an example of a tracking sheet, prepared on the computer:
If you complete it on a computer, you can easily update it as changes are made. It helps to date it, so you know if it is the most recent version.

EVITA: ALEKS PEVEC
09.08.12
DRESS SL HALLWAY FOR TOP OF SHOW

ACT I

REQUIEM
Start in 2nd line between BD and MF w/ candle and cross (cross in jacket pocket)
Finish in most US line
Lift both arms on 5th "Evita" as lines arrive, and bring arms down before 2nd Req

OH WHAT A CIRCUS
Stay standing in spot for most of song
Turn to face US on "Pretty bad state for a state to be in' & BH will come to you
Hug BH on "one who's died"
Mourning tango w/ BH in 3rd line SL2
Do bolero x4 (cheat DS after 2nd boleo)
Exit out stage SL catacomb

COSTUME CHANGE INTO WORKER IN SL HALLWAY

BUENOS AIRES
Follow LH for entrance snake.
Follow CG US to be opposite MAGALDI in window of BH & EVA
Face US 1st time
Walk DSR diagonal into SR triangle, keeping US of AS
DS point of triangle
Follow MAGALDI to "mountain" position
2nd in window between AS & EVA for "Mountain"
Turn back on self to loop around MAGALDI and follow him into DSR triangle
DS point of triangle
Follow MAGALDI to mountain position
Walk on spot to get in position for circle
3rd circle going clockwise following MD
1st link: 7 o'clock with LH and BL
2nd link: 1 o'clock with KC and RE
Pinwheel: at 9 o'clock
Walk DS and loop back in to be in front line between KC and M for workers speech
Follow RP to travel to US of group
Stand on outside of KDS R shoulder for military speech
Follow KDS to travel to middle of group
Stand behind KDS for aristo speech
Follow NK DS to loop around EVA for partnering break finishing SR on DS of NK
1st eight in place
Cross SL to be US of CG by overhead lift
Walk SR towards center by the time JS starts partnering
Have moment w/ MAGALDI
Partner SR side of EVA for trio w/ NK
SL side of EVA for six men w/ EVA
L side of T lift grabbing shoulder and arm
Travel DS to 1st line between EVA and ER for lunges, starting L foot first
Follow ER for snake
Travel straight DS for button

BUENOS AIRES PLAYOFF
Partner EVA for play off and exit USL w/ her for Lovers

GOOD NIGHT AND THANK YOU
Get kimono offstage at top of spiral stairs and walk US to inside of apartment
Close door behind EVA as she steps out on balcony

Here is an example of a track sheet before it's finalized for the show bible. The dance captain prints off the temporary, draft version and then adds detailed notes when they *trail* or discuss the track with the actor. Again, the more information, the better. In this example, the dance captain added backstage notes, traffic notes and tips to help her be more specific.

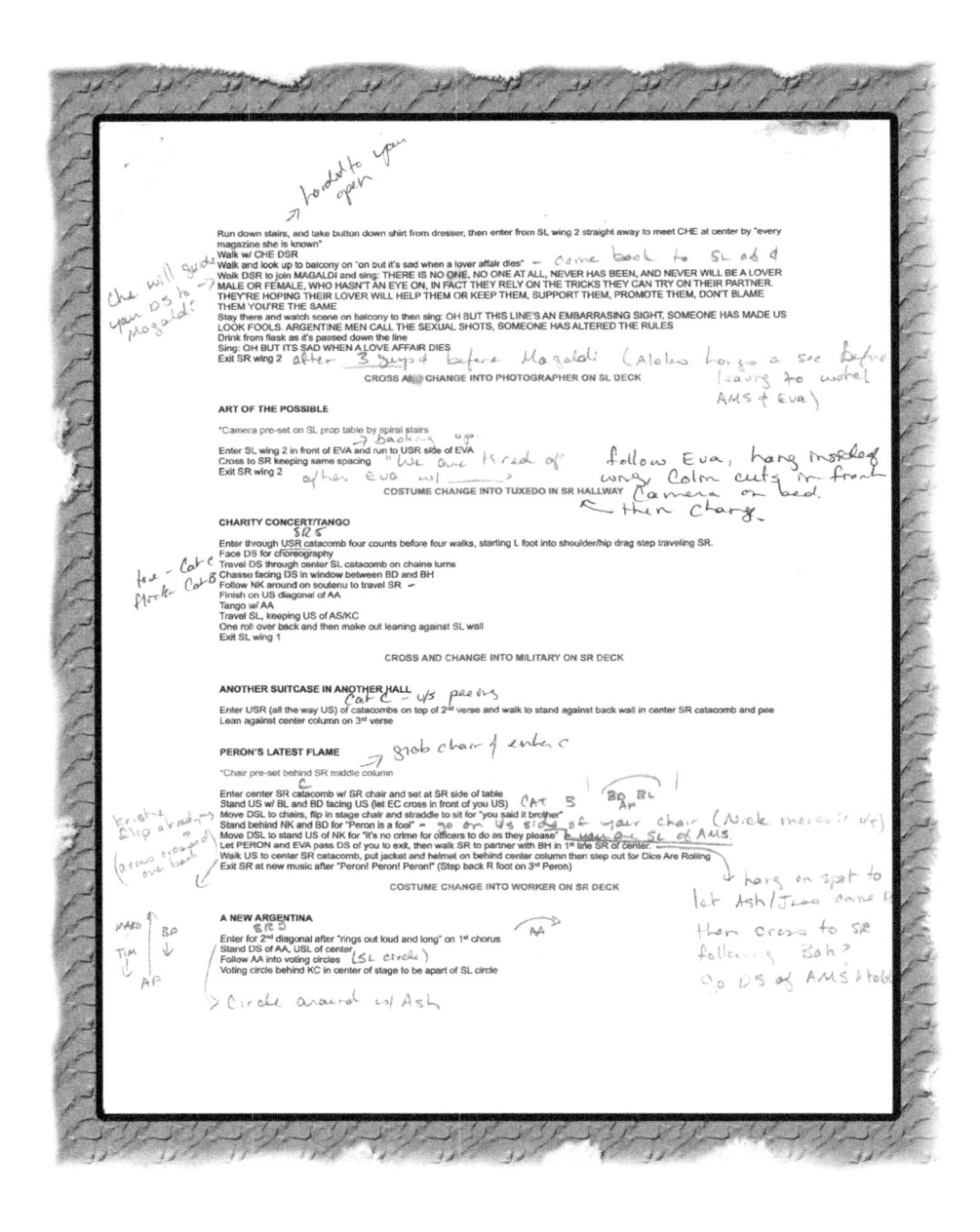

[handwritten note at top: "lord to to you open"]
[handwritten arrow with "backing"]

Run down stairs, and take button down shirt from dresser, then enter from SL wing 2 straight away to meet CHE at center by "every magazine she is known"
Walk w/ CHE DSR
Walk and look up to balcony on "on but it's sad when a lover affair dies" — *come back to SL ad d*
Walk DSR to join MAGALDI and sing: THERE IS NO ONE, NO ONE AT ALL, NEVER HAS BEEN, AND NEVER WILL BE A LOVER MALE OR FEMALE, WHO HASN'T AN EYE ON, IN FACT THEY RELY ON THE TRICKS THEY CAN TRY ON THEIR PARTNER. THEY'RE HOPING THEIR LOVER WILL HELP THEM OR KEEP THEM, SUPPORT THEM, PROMOTE THEM, DON'T BLAME THEM YOU'RE THE SAME

[left margin: "Che will guide you DS to Magaldi"]

Stay there and watch scene on balcony to then sing: OH BUT THIS LINE'S AN EMBARRASSING SIGHT, SOMEONE HAS MADE US LOOK FOOLS. ARGENTINE MEN CALL THE SEXUAL SHOTS, SOMEONE HAS ALTERED THE RULES
Drink from flask as it's passed down the line
Sing: OH BUT ITS SAD WHEN A LOVE AFFAIR DIES
Exit SR wing 2 *after 3 guys d before Magaldi (Aleks hangs a sec before leaving to model AMS & EVA)*

CROSS AND CHANGE INTO PHOTOGRAPHER ON SL DECK

ART OF THE POSSIBLE

*Camera pre-set on SL prop table by spiral stairs   *up.*
Enter SL wing 2 in front of EVA and run to USR side of EVA *backing*
Cross to SR keeping same spacing *"we are tired of"* → *follow Eva, hang modeled*
Exit SR wing 2 *after Eva w/___*   *wing Colm cuts in front*
                                                       Camera on bed
COSTUME CHANGE INTO TUXEDO IN SR HALLWAY   ← *then charg.*

CHARITY CONCERT/TANGO *SR S*
Enter through USR catacomb four counts before four walks, starting L foot into shoulder/hip drag step traveling SR.
Face DS for choreography
Travel DS through center SL catacomb on chaine turns
Chasse facing DS in window between BD and BH
Follow NK around on soutenu to travel SR
Finish on US diagonal of AA
Tango w/ AA
Travel SL, keeping US of AS/KC
One roll over back and then make out leaning against SL wall
Exit SL wing 1

[left margin: "toe - Cat C   Flick - Cat B"]

CROSS AND CHANGE INTO MILITARY ON SR DECK

ANOTHER SUITCASE IN ANOTHER HALL *Cat C — u/s peeing*
Enter USR (all the way US) of catacombs on top of 2nd verse and walk to stand against back wall in center SR catacomb and pee
Lean against center column on 3rd verse

PERON'S LATEST FLAME   → *grab chair & enter c*
*Chair pre-set behind SR middle column
Enter center SR catacomb w/ SR chair and set at SR side of table *CAT 3*   *BD BL*
Stand US w/ BL and BD facing US (let EC cross in front of you US)   *AP*
Move DSL to chairs, flip in stage chair and straddle to sit for "you said it brother"
Stand behind NK and BD for "Peron is a fool" — *go on US side of your chair (Nick moves it up)*
Move DSL to stand US of NK for "It's no crime for officers to do as they please" *SL of AMS*
Let PERON and EVA pass DS of you to exit, then walk SR to partner with BH in 1st line SR of center.
Walk US to center SR catacomb, put jacket and helmet on behind center column then step out for Dice Are Rolling
Exit SR at new music after "Peron! Peron! Peron!" (Step back R foot on 3rd Peron)

[right margin: "hang on spot to let Ash/Jess come b then cross to SR following Boh? go DS of AMS & tab"]
[left margin: "Kristie already step already (arms crossed out back"]

COSTUME CHANGE INTO WORKER ON SR DECK

A NEW ARGENTINA *SR S*
Enter for 2nd diagonal after "rings out loud and long" on 1st chorus   *AA*
Stand DS of AA, USL of center
Follow AA into voting circles   *(SL circle)*
Voting circle behind KC in center of stage to be apart of SL circle

[left margin: "MARO ↑ BP   TIM ↓   L   AP"]
→ *Circle around w/ Ash*

- Making a Show Bible -

Here is an example of the same track sheet, after it's been cleaned up. The dance captain incorporated all the added pencil notes to her original. She kept these permanent tracking sheets in the bible and referred to them every time she had to teach that particular track.

Run down stairs, and take button down shirt (dresser hands it to you as you come down the stairs) then enter from SL2 straight away to meet CHE at center by "every magazine she is known"
Put shirt on during Che's solo
Che will guide you DSR on "...but we don't always answer..."
Walk back to SL of center and look up to balcony on "on but it's sad when a love affair dies..."
Walk DSR to join MAGALDI

Vocal: "THERE IS NO ONE, NO ONE AT ALL, NEVER HAS BEEN, AND NEVER WILL BE A LOVER MALE OR FEMALE, WHO HASN'T AN EYE ON, IN FACT THEY RELY ON THE TRICKS THEY CAN TRY ON THEIR PARTNER. THEY'RE HOPING THEIR LOVER WILL HELP THEM OR KEEP THEM, SUPPORT THEM, PROMOTE THEM, DON'T BLAME THEM YOU'RE THE SAME"

Stay there and watch scene on balcony to then sing: "OH BUT THIS LINE'S AN EMBARRASSING SIGHT, SOMEONE HAS MADE US LOOK FOOLS. ARGENTINE MEN CALL THE SEXUAL SHOTS, SOMEONE HAS ALTERED THE RULES"
Drink from flask as it's passed down the line
Sing: "OH BUT ITS SAD WHEN A LOVE AFFAIR DIES"
Exit SR2 following CC (Hang out for a second to watch Eva and Alex before exiting)

CROSS AND CHANGE INTO PHOTOGRAPHER ON SL DECK

ART OF THE POSSIBLE
*Camera pre-set on SL prop table by spiral stairs
Enter SL2 in front of EVA (backing up) and run to USR side of EVA
Cross to SR ("We are tired of") keeping same spacing
Exit SR2 (follow Eva, hang inside of wing, Colin cuts in front then place camera on the bed on your way to QC.

COSTUME CHANGE INTO TUXEDO IN SR HALLWAY

CHARITY CONCERT/TANGO
Enter through USR5 catacomb four counts before four walks, starting L foot into shoulder/hip drag step traveling SR.
Face DS for choreography
Travel DS through catacomb C on chaine turns (toe touch happens in catacomb B)
Chasse facing DS in window between BD and BH
Follow NK around on soutenu to travel SR
Finish on USL diagonal of AA
Tango w/ AA
Travel SL, keeping US of AS/KC
One roll over back and then make out leaning against SL wall
Exit SL wing 1

CROSS AND CHANGE INTO MILITARY ON SR DECK

ANOTHER SUITCASE IN ANOTHER HALL
Enter USR (all the way US) of catacombs on top of 2nd verse & walk to stand against back wall in catacomb C to pee
Lean against center column on 3rd verse

PERON'S LATEST FLAME
*Chair pre-set behind SR middle column
Enter catacomb C w/ SR chair and set at SR side of table   BD   BL
Stand US in catacomb B w/ BL and BD facing US (let EC cross in front of you US   AP
Move DSL to chairs and straddle to sit for "you said it brother" (arms folded across chair back)
Stand behind NK and BD for "Peron is a fool" (be on US side of your chair just SL of AMS)
Follow BD DSL to end standing SR of BD for "it's no crime for officers to do as they please"
Let PERON and EVA pass DS of you to exit. Hang on the spot to let AA and JP come DS, then cross to SR following BH (stay DS of AMS and the table) to partner with BH in 1st line SR of center.
Walk US to catacomb C (SR of BD and SL of TS and MDB), put jacket and helmet on behind center column then step out SR for Dice Are Rolling
Exit SR at new music after "Peron! Peron! Peron!" (Step back R foot on 3rd Peron)

COSTUME CHANGE INTO WORKER ON SR DECK

Stage Write

      Stage Write is an application for an ipad that became available in 2012. The creator, Jeff Whiting, worked with Susan Stroman on a number of Broadway shows. He was her associate director and recognized a need to digitalize Broadway show bibles and create a standard. It allows for a clean, easy-to-read bible that is easy to share. Since it's release, it's already been embraced by the entertainment community and is being used by over 50 Broadway and National Tour productions, as well as theaters around the globe.

      There are two "app" programs for a Broadway bible. The first is *Stage Write* and the companion app is *Staging Score*, also written by Jeff Whiting. Stage Write is a program to make charts for your bible.

      On Stage Write, you can insert the stage dimensions, the actors, the set pieces and other information you need to make a chart. There are a lot of great things you can do with the app, such as put all your actors in "the green room". You can give each actor a shape, a color, and name.

- Making a Show Bible - 85

Below are examples of the actors being put into the "greenroom" and creating set pieces. You can choose what shape (square, circle, diamond), color and lettering you want for "Leo". You can choose "stock set pieces" (bed, chair) for a scene or create your own.

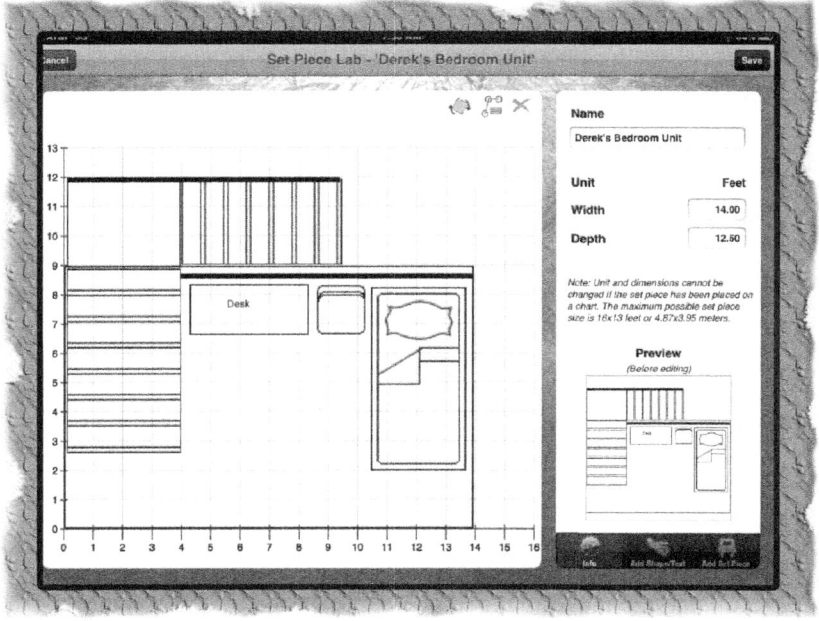

Below are examples of charts done in Stage Write:

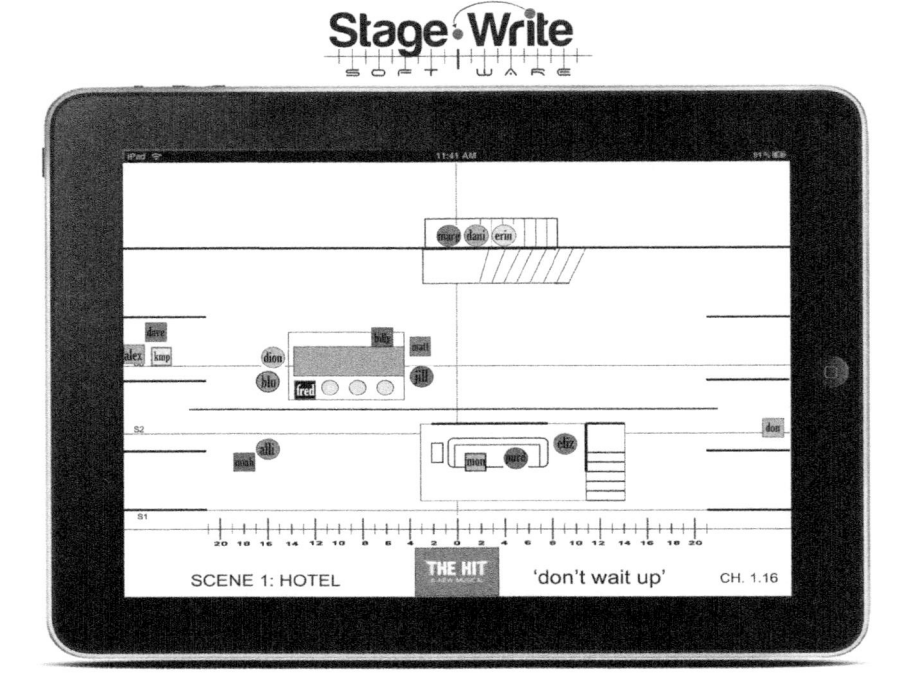

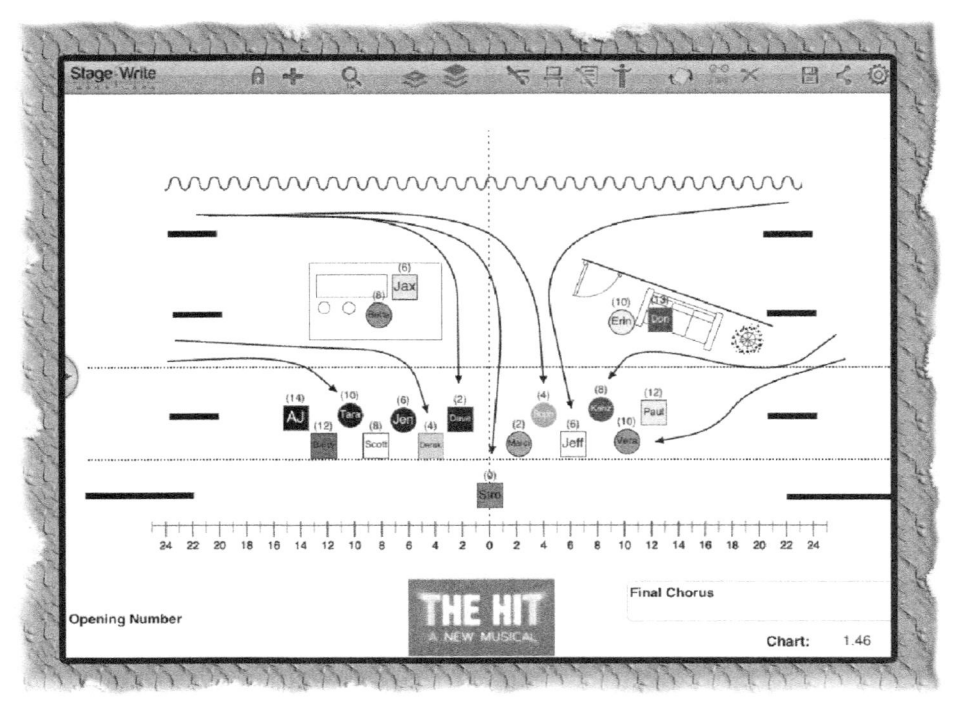

- Making a Show Bible - 87

Below is an example of a chart that was hand written. To the right of the handwritten chart is an example of the same chart done on the Stage Write app. As you can see, it's much clearer to see the details.

which would you choose?

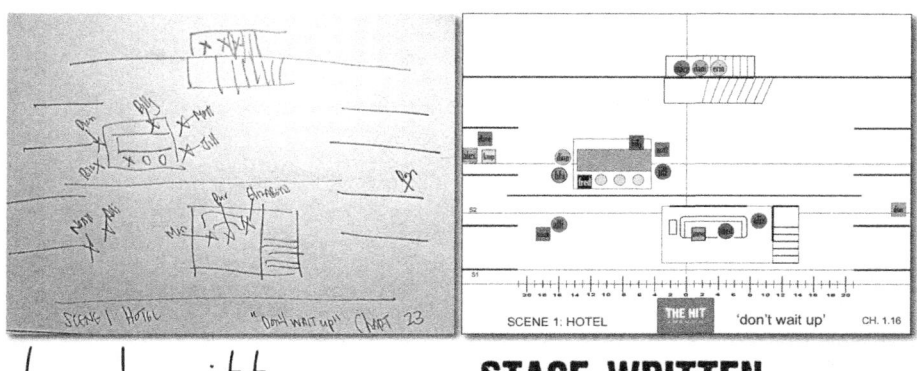

hand-written...   **STAGE-WRITTEN...**

Stage Write is a great way to notate charts but it's really only half of the information you need to make a show bible. To have a more detailed show bible, you really need to have the choreography and staging written down too.

SPACING CHARTS + STAGING SCORE
─────────────────
SHOW BIBLE

Staging Score

Staging Score is a program (an app) to make the staging notes and notate choreography for your bible. It works in tandem with Stage Write charts to more fully document staging and choreography. Jeff called it "Staging Score" because he found it similar to a score in music.

Much like a conductor can look at an orchestral score and see what each instrument is playing on every beat, Staging Score allows you to document all the actions and choreography for all performers and technical elements, in as much or as little detail as you want to share, and yet is still aligned by the counts or timing so you can easily see what every person (or element) is doing at a glance. The method works whether there are musical counts, or not. You can use the two programs together and link staging notes to the corresponding chart.

In the pages ahead, you will see many examples of how to use Staging Score and Stage Write. We do not go into detail about how to input everything into the app, but it will give you an overview of what to expect with the app.

- Making a Show Bible -

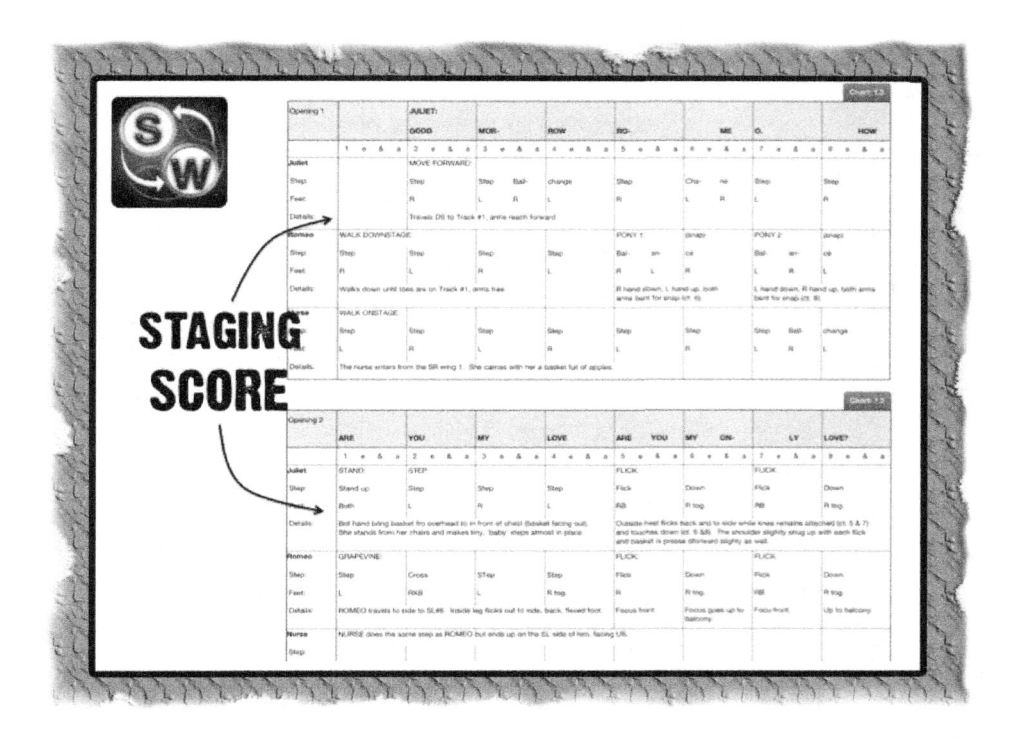

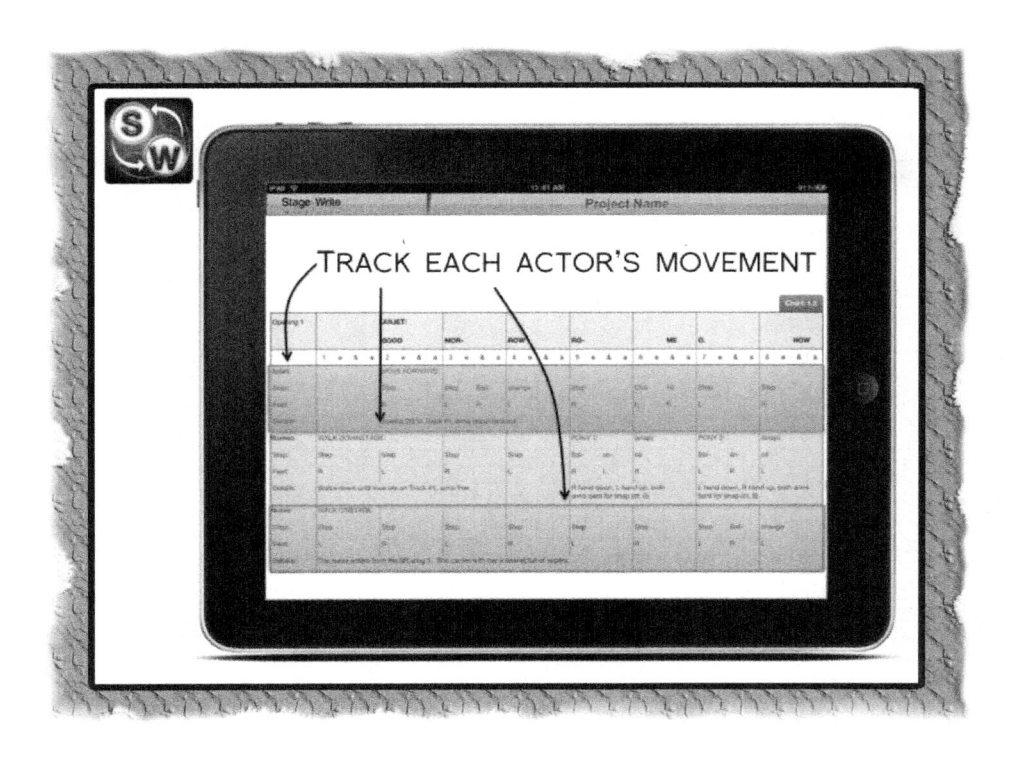

STAGING SCORE

TRACK EACH ACTOR'S MOVEMENT

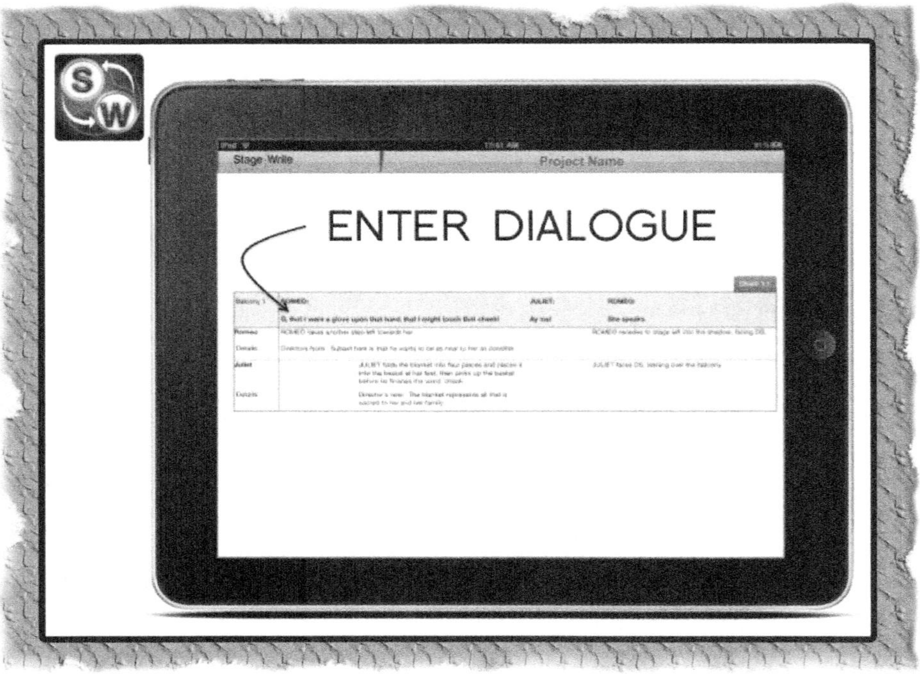
Stage Write
Project Name
ENTER DIALOGUE

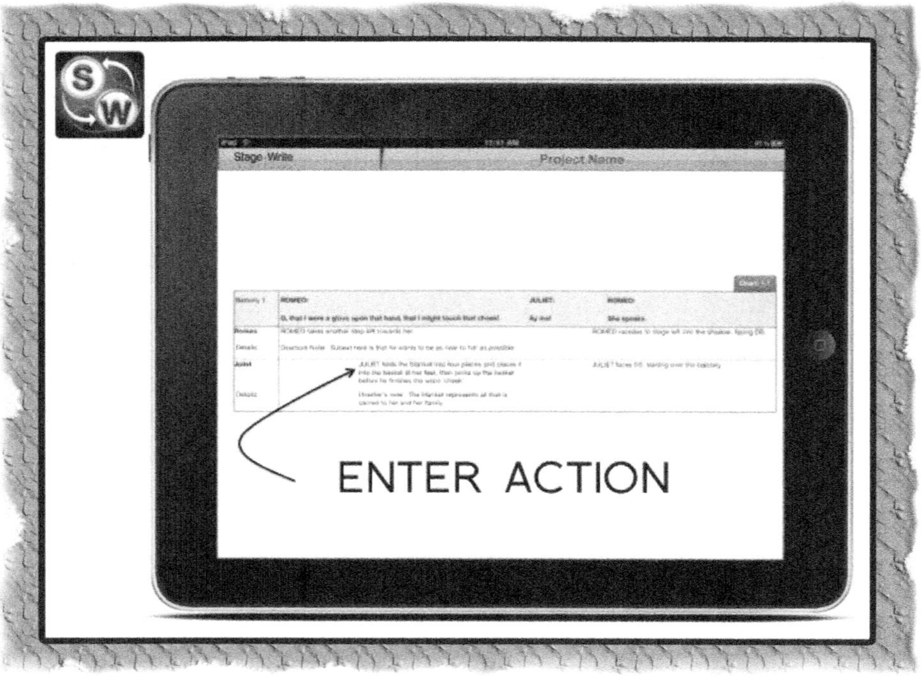
Stage Write
Project Name
ENTER ACTION

- Making a Show Bible -   91

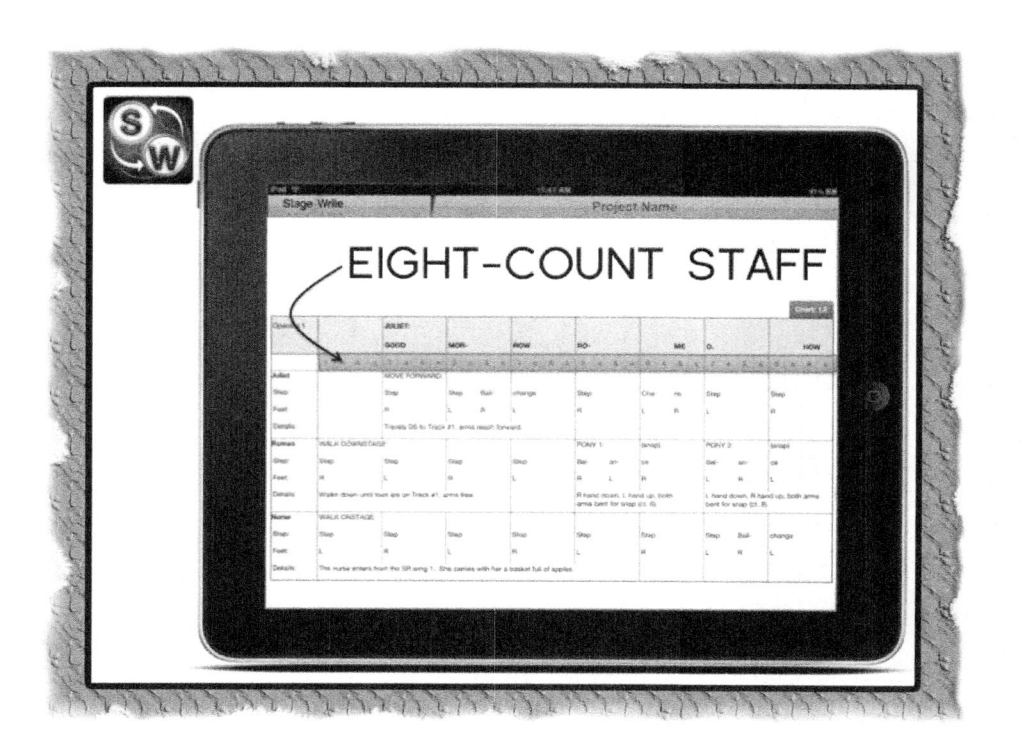

92 - Be the best *DANCE CAPTAIN* on Broadway -

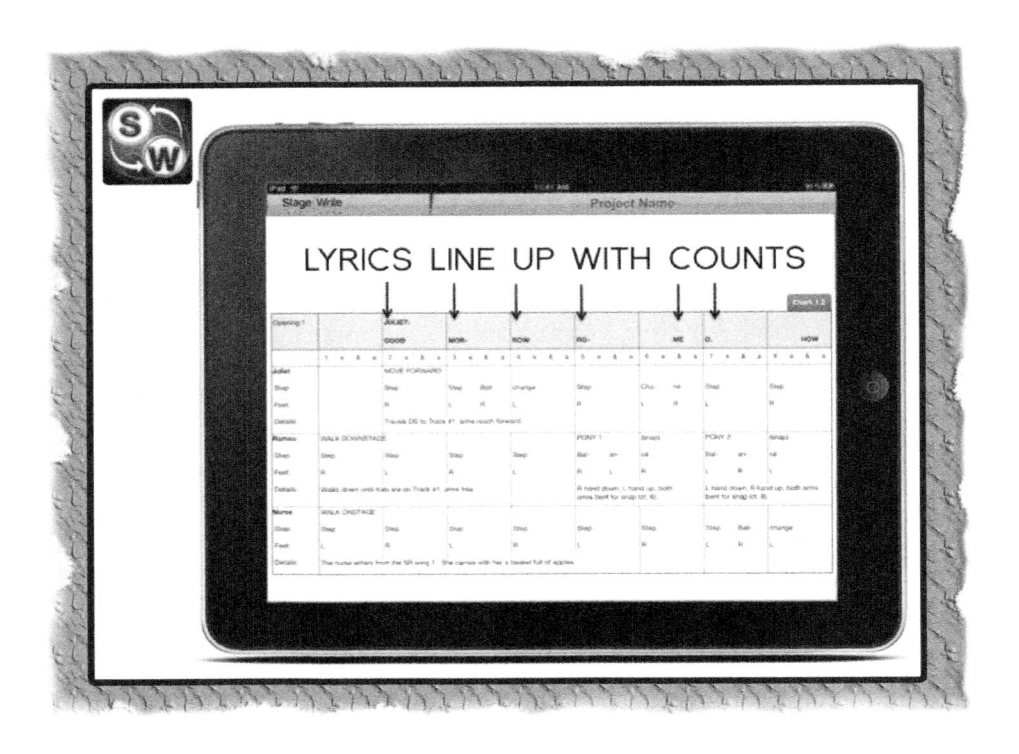

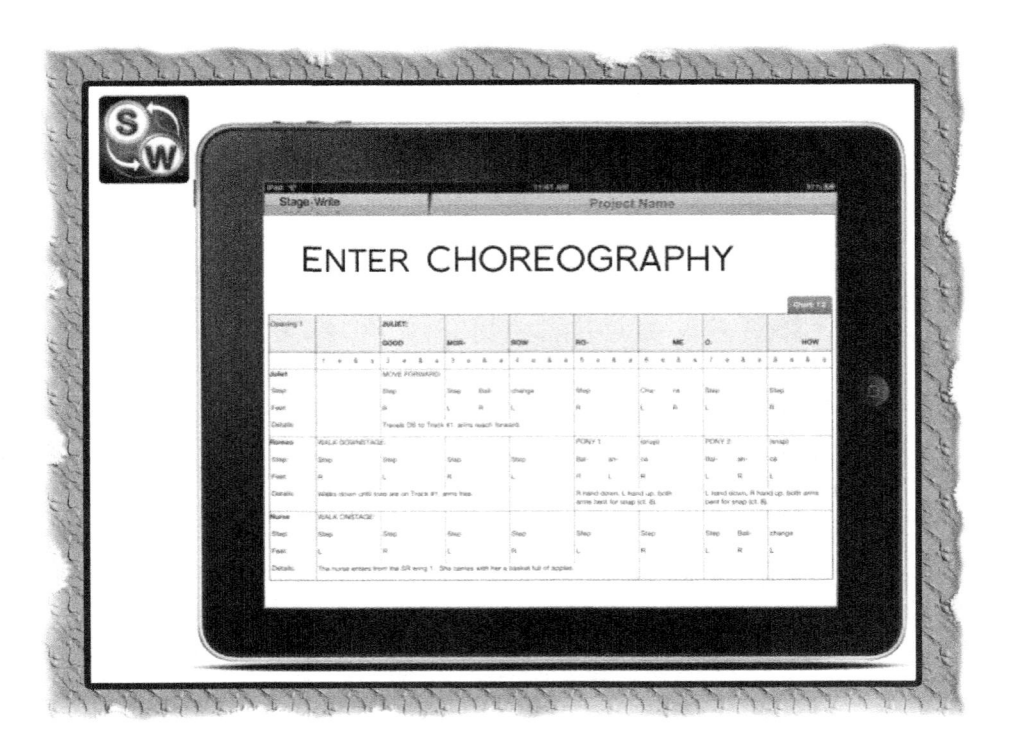

You link Stage Score to the corresponding Stage Write chart to make a show bible.

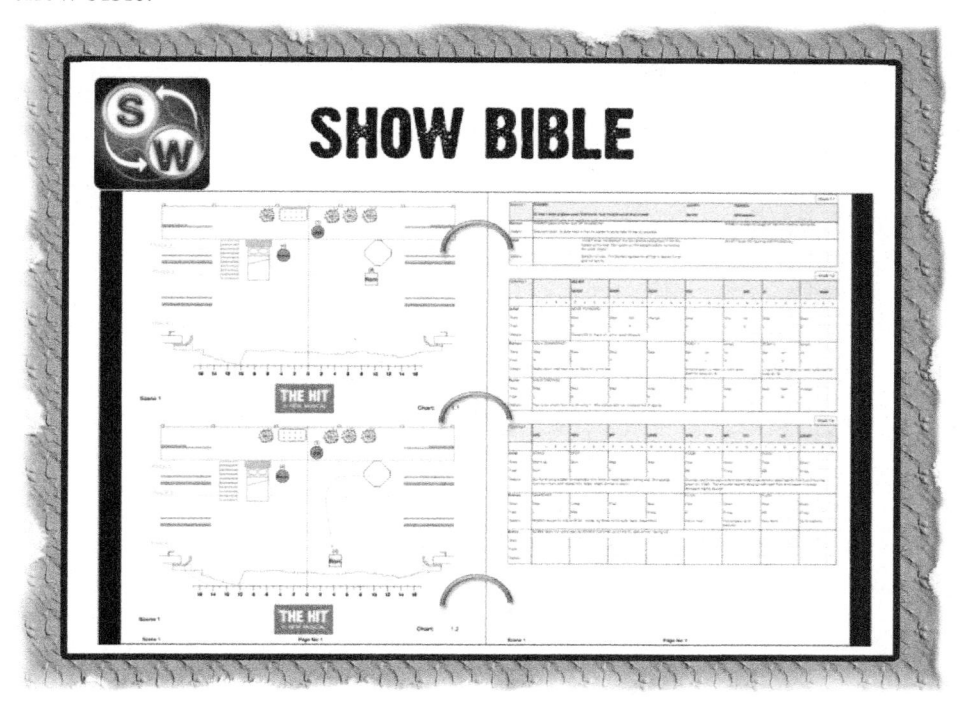

As you can see from the example above, Stage write provides a great way to digitize a show bible. To find out more about this app, visit www.stagewritesoftware.com. You can also find detailed videos on You Tube on how to use the app and input information.

Using photos, video and audio recordings for bible

There are certain aids that can assist you in creating a bible. If you watch the show once, you are likely to obtain a limited amount of information for your book. You have to watch a show over and over and over to receive all the needed information. If you teach understudy rehearsal, you may not have the luxury of time to watch many shows before rehearsal. A video is handy in this case. With video, you can watch it many times in short order to clarify traffic patterns, see what all 30 actors are doing at any given moment, entrance and exits, props handling, and clarify music counts.

This is a tricky subject because you are working in a union show. There are many unions that the cast, crew, and *creatives* belong to that guard against recording of any kind to protect their work. A choreographer may not want to have his choreography "ripped of" or a set designer may not want his designs to be photographed for others to use. An actor may also have an issue with being filmed in case they are not performing his/her best that day. People get nervous when they don't have control over what happens to that video. There are ways to gather information using audio and recording devices but you must be cognisant of protocols and use the method sparingly.

Actors' Equity now allows the taping of rehearsal footage with notice to the company and the union. The taping of the entire show is often done on the last day(s) of the rehearsal process in the studio. This is without lights, sets, costumes, and orchestra. It is a "wide-shot" video and is used for such things as the lighting designer getting a better idea of what the patterns are to pre-light a show before the cast comes in. This saves time and ultimately money during tech rehearsals. The dance captain is allowed to use this type of footage to help assist him/her also. The dance captain cannot use this footage in place of teaching an understudy or for giving notes and reprimanding actors for mistakes. This is a great way to get specifics down in your bible in a quick manner.

> TIP:
> ONLY use video and audio recordings you need to do your job for the show. There are union rules for protection reasons and you have to respect why they are there. Do not share, post, make CD's or DVD's, or do anything other than look at it for learning purposes. Treat it with the utmost care and respect.

Often the dance captain or swings can be seen in the rehearsal room taking quick videos of traffic patterns or such to help them. However, it would be better to have one or two people do the taping and share as necessary so it doesn't appear like paparazzi to the cast, making them feel uneasy and ruining anyone's chances of taking video.

It's also helpful to get the audio recording of a song to help set up your staging notes and learn how to count each number. If a choreographer counts the choreography a certain way, then it's helpful if you count the same way. For example, in EVITA, there were times when the choreography was counted 1-8, then 1-7, and even 1-10! If you run a put-in and you count the choreography differently than the choreographer did, it will confuse the cast and waste time.

Another helpful tool is a photo to help you with stage positions. For example, actors may be given specific poses for the button of a number and you may want to get a picture so you can be accurate when teaching those tracks. It's a lot quicker to take a quick picture than draw 30 stick figures!

If you are in a new show, there will likely be many changes to the show between rehearsal and opening night. What can you do about those changes? It's a lot more tricky when you get to the theatre and add costumes, sets, lights and props. You won't be able to walk around with a video recorder anytime you want. Each union member will feel very strongly about this and rightly so.

You have a job to do and taking videos of the things you need can help you and the show if you were to be thrown on. You may want to sit in the balcony or somewhere that is not obvious to get what you need. You also want to make sure there are no lights or anything that would be distracting while you are obtaining what you need.

Once the show is in previews, you will not be able to tape anything during those shows. Any recording of changes would need to be done in rehearsal that day. Again, if there are swings that need the same information, "divide and conquer" rather than have a whole army of people trying to look inconspicuous.

TIP:
Press can KILL a show! Keep it "in the room".

In the present day of social media, everyone has to be overly protective of what they put out into the world. If a new show is rehearsing, many people will be wondering what it's like. Others want to know if it will be in competition with their show, if it's good, if there is drama behind the scenes and so forth. Even an innocent conversation with a friend regarding how the choreographer got mad at an actor, can turn into unpleasant and unwelcome attention to the show. It causes the public to form an opinion about the show based on what they've heard or seen prematurely.

It's amazing how many people have an opinion about a show even before they see it and they share that opinion with others. The audience should only have an opinion once they have attended the show. Don't jeopardize the show or your job by leaking gossip, videos, audio recordings, or pictures before it's allowed. There is nothing worse than being blogged about for weeks before the first preview. Treat it with the same respect you would a surprise party. Let the anticipation be part of the joy the audience experiences before they see the show. Experiment with what "hype" and "privacy" can do for a show. "Surprise" is a powerful tool! It will put more butts in the seats and help the success of your show.

CHAPTER 10

Rehearsals

There are certain rules in the Production Contract that define how often the dance captain is allowed to rehearse before he/she is entitled to overtime payment. This is something that is negotiated by the union and can change with each term of the Production Contract. Find out the most recent dance captain rules at www.actorsequity.org. You will find the information under "document library", then "agreement", then "Production Rulebook" ("League" or "Disney", depending on who is your employer).

The number of allowable hours is dictated by whether or not a show has officially opened to the public yet. Most shows only have one day off per week, so you can expect to work 6 days a week.

Here are the current maximum rehearsal hours a dance captain can expect:

1. During rehearsal, prior to the first public performance: All actors must not exceed 7 hours of rehearsal over a span of 8 and a half hours. This means you could rehearse from 10am-6pm with an hour lunch break. Or, you could rehearse from 9:30am-6:00pm with an hour and a half lunch break. They can start the rehearsal anytime of the day as long as you only rehearse 7 hours during the span of 8 ½ hours. You could even rehearse 2:00pm-10:00pm with an hour dinner break.
2. The final 7 days of rehearsal prior to the first public performance: The producers may shift to *10-out-of-12* rehearsals. This means that they can rehearse you for 10 hours over the span of 12 hours. They often do

this during *tech*, before a show opens to the public. A typical rehearsal schedule may be: rehearse 12:00-5:00pm, break for dinner 5:00-6:30pm, rehearse 6:30pm-11:30pm.
3. During previews: There are some options producers can utilize regarding rehearsal hours once the show is in previews. These options are too numerous to list here. Check the specifics at www.actorsequity.org in the Production Contract under "rehearsals". Generally, you will rehearse 4 or 5 hours in the afternoon and then do a show. There may be a note session in the theatre after the performance. On two show days, you will not likely have rehearsal but you may have a note session before or after the performances.
4. After the *official opening*, the dance captain's hours are limited to 12 hours per week. The hours you rehearse during a show do not count towards the 12. They are allowed to ask you to rehearse starting at half hour up until the show is done and it doesn't count as part of your 12 hours.

Overtime

Overtime is paid when a dance captain is asked to rehearse "outside" the allotted hours. The overtime rate is negotiated in the Production Contract and can change each term. Check www.actorsequity.org for the current overtime rates. As of 2015, the overtime rate was $45/hour.

Overtime will be paid if you are asked to rehearse:
1) More than the weekly rehearsal hours (12 hours after opening)
2) The *day after the day off*
3) The *day off*

Day after the day off:
There are two scenarios with different payments. It depends if you are rehearsing a replacement actor or an understudy. In one scenario, you get *straight overtime* with a minimum 4 hour call. The other scenario, you get *time and a half* without a minimum amount of hours. It gets even more complicated if you have a combination of the two types of rehearsal.

If a dance captain is called to rehearse a *replacement actor* or run an audition on the *day after the day off,* he/she will be paid straight overtime for those hours, with a minimum of 4 hours. *Straight overtime* is defined as the overtime rate for one hour. For example, if a dance captain has to run an audition for 2 hours, then he/she will be paid 4 hours of overtime.

If a dance captain is called to rehearse for any other reason, such as working with an *understudy,* then he/she would be paid *time and a half*. *Time and a half* is 1.5 times the overtime rate for every hour rehearsed. There is no minimum of hours. You could be called to rehearse with the understudy for one hour in this scenario and only be paid for one hour.

If a dance captain is called to rehearse a replacement for part of the day and an understudy for another part of the day, there would be a 4 hour minimum. He/she would be paid *time and a half* for the rehearsal with the understudy and s*traight time* for rehearsal with the replacement.

In the above scenarios, hours paid do not count towards the 12 hours of rehearsal during the week. These are "over and above" because you are already getting overtime to rehearse.

The *day off*:
There is no provision in the rule book for working on the day off because it is expected that you will not have to work that day. There may be a small chance you get asked to run an audition. If so, Equity would likely make a claim that you should be paid *double overtime* with a 4 hour minimum call.

Exception to the overtime rule:
If the show moves to another theatre or there are major cast changes, the company can be called for a put-in without compensation. You would not be entitled to overtime. "Major cast changes" are defined as putting in a star, major featured principal, or three or more chorus.

Weekly Rehearsals

You will have ongoing weekly rehearsals after a show opens. Along with the stage manager, you will be required to teach swings, understudies and replacement actors. Depending on the show schedule, you will likely have one or two afternoons per week dedicated for this. Most commonly, you will rehearse from 1:00-5:00pm or 12:00-5:00pm on those days. If you are teaching a replacement actor, you will be rehearsing every day, except the day off.

How to run a weekly rehearsal

Actors will come to rehearsal and expect to be taught their parts. You should know how you want to run the rehearsal and what the best use of everyone's time will be. Each rehearsal week will be different depending on who needs rehearsing. At the beginning of a new show, all the understudies and swings need a lot of rehearsal. After the show is open for some time, there may be just a replacement actor or a few understudies that need to learn something. Then, ongoing, there are swings and understudies who need to keep practising what they learned already.

Who teaches what?

You will be working with the stage manager and the musical director to teach the swings, understudies and replacements. Usually the music department will want to make sure an actor knows what lyrics and parts to sing before doing anything else. A music rehearsal is likely one of the first rehearsals an actor will have. Once the music information is given to an actor, he/she can practise singing at home in his/her own time too.

A stage manager will need time with an actor to teach them all the scenes and blocking for the musical. If there is a lot of scene work, the stage manager may call a rehearsal and not need you to be there to teach choreography. It really differs from show to show depending on how much choreography or scene work is in the show.

Who will be there?

In most Broadway shows, there are multiple understudies and swings for each role. You will have to decide, along with the stage manager and musical director, how you want to handle teaching the understudies. Will you have all understudies there or just one set of understudies? What is most beneficial to the understudies and most effective way for you to teach them? Some shows decide to have both sets of understudies at rehearsal, especially if everyone needs to learn their roles and just gather information to get them started. This allows for all understudies to learn the information in case they were to be "thrown on". For example, if a principal gets sick and one understudy is out, the other understudy will be asked to perform. It doesn't matter how much or little rehearsal the actor has had. It's in everyone's interest to get the information as soon as possible. Some shows do not enumerate the understudies (name who is first or second understudy), so it's a good way to teach everyone quickly and see which understudy is most comfortable in the role.

> *TIP:*
> *If you are thinking about calling in the understudies to rehearse at the same time, it's a good idea to have a conversation with each understudy to see if he/she is comfortable with the idea. Some actors don't want the pressure of being watched or judged while they are learning. It's a very vulnerable position to be in. On the other hand, some understudies just want to get the information as quickly as possible and are fine with rehearsing all together. In some situations, the stage manager and dance captain will call both sets of understudies to learn the blocking and choreography, but the understudies will not be expected to do it or perform it (sing a solo, act, or dance) in that type of rehearsal. They would wait for a future rehearsal, after they have had a chance to practise more and are not surrounded by all the understudies at once.*

Swings are often called to all the rehearsals because of how many tracks they cover. Any practise time onstage is beneficial to swings. There may come a time when the swings feel more comfortable in their tracks and don't need to be at all the rehearsals. Evaluate as you go. Just because swings *can* be called doesn't mean they *should* be. You want to create a positive relationship with all swings and you don't want them to feel "used". If they are called for rehearsal, make sure it's useful for them. It is similar with the full company called to rehearse. Technically they can be called in to rehearse for up to 8 hours a week. If this happened on a regular basis, on top of their show schedule, you would find a very unhappy company. It's just too mentally and physically demanding to be working continuously.

What will you teach?

There are two ways to teach understudies, swings and replacement actors.
1. Start at the top of the show and work your way through.
2. Start with the most technical aspect of their show and make sure they are comfortable with those sections before teaching the rest.

This decision will differ from show to show. If there are technically demanding aspects (out of the actor's comfort zone), it may be better to give additional time to those. This gives the actor more time to practise and get familiar with the difficulties. It's a good idea to check in with your swings and understudies to see what they are worried about the most and hoping to practise. This will give you a better idea of how to run the most effective and useful rehearsal.

> *"Our rehearsals were so unfocused and often a disaster and complete waste of time. Neither the dance captain nor the stage manager ever took the time to really address specific needs of the swings and understudies. They just made their own assessment of the parts they thought were tricky. We would waste about 20 minutes of valuable rehearsal time just trying to figure out how we were actually going to rehearse, or who was going to do which parts and sections. Worst of all, we were often missing props or the right crew to rehearse those specific sections. Had the dance captain created some sort of outreach to the understudies and swings, she would've been able to address the specific needs and concerns of all of us. Had there been a little pre-planning on what needed rehearsing and how we would do it, we would have been more efficient and prepared."*
>
> \- Anonymous swing

An example of a typical rehearsal week (working with understudies):

The rehearsals for an understudy typically happen on Thursdays and Fridays every week if the show has a typical performance schedule of two shows on Wednesday and two shows on Saturday. If you are rehearsing an understudy who is already in the show (doing his/her own track), the musical director might have an hour or two with the actor to teach them the vocal parts of the song they have to understudy. Because they are in the show, they already know most of the songs in the show from previous rehearsals. Then, the stage manager might work with the understudy for a couple hours and teach the entrances, exits, props used, blocking and character's intentions. Once the music and staging is taught, the dance captain would teach any choreography and musical staging the understudy needs to learn for the role he/she covers.

Thursday: 1-3pm understudy with the musical director (music)
            1-5pm understudy with the stage manager (blocking)
Friday: 1-5pm understudy with the dance captain (choreography)

When you have multiple understudies at the same time, the rehearsals are staggered throughout each day because each understudy has to learn something different. The musical director, stage manager and dance captain will figure out the most efficient way of scheduling, depending on who needs to learn what.

Thursday: 1-2pm understudy #1 with musical director (music)
2-3pm understudy #2 with musical director (music)
3-4pm understudy #3 with musical director (music)
4-5pm understudy #4 with musical director (music)
1-3pm understudy #3 and #4 with stage manager (blocking)
3-5pm understudy #1 and #2 with stage manager (blocking)

Friday: 1-3pm understudy #1 and #2 with dance captain (choreography)
3-5pm understudy #3 and #4 with dance captain (choreography)

Once the understudies have learned all they need to, they will start having one rehearsal per week (or every other week) where they just practise the show and basically run through it with props and scenery. In this case, each role will only have one understudy perform the role. The other "set" (of understudies) will have another rehearsal day to run the show.

> *TIP:*
> *Don't make one set of understudies watch the run-through of the other understudies. This allows for much needed rest for the company after performing regularly at night. There have been some stage managers who asked the other set to come in and watch, but it often makes actors upset (both watching and being watched). Each understudy likes to bring his/her own character to a role and doesn't want to be influenced by watching another understudy do the role.*

An example of a typical rehearsal week (working with swings):

The swings are often hired at the beginning of the rehearsal process for a new show and learn the choreography and music with everyone else. The main purpose of the weekly rehearsal for swings is getting the chance to do it on the stage and answer any remaining questions they have about tracks they cover. Some swings will need more teaching than others. Some swings come from a singing background, or dancing or acting, and need more practise with the other disciplines.

The best way to rehearse swings is to ask each one what they need and what would make the best use of their time. Have the swings make a list of all the things they want to rehearse or need answers to. Examples might be: learning the choreography of a number, practising a dance lift they never get to practise, having access to props or scenery they are worried about, learning the harmonies of a song where they have to cover multiple parts. Once you have an overall idea of what the swings need, you can decide how to rehearse with them weekly. You may need to stagger the calls at the beginning if there is a lot of new information to give them. For example, you may want to call in the male swings for two hours, separate from the girls, if they have different things to learn. Or perhaps the stage manager could be working with the female swings using props and scenery while you teach dancing to the male swings. Each show will have different rehearsal needs and each week's rehearsal needs will change as the swings become more comfortable with their tracks. It's good to integrate the swings and the understudies in other rehearsals too. The more people onstage the better, for all involved. It gives a better sense of the show.

Thursday: 1-3pm Male swings with dance captain (choreography)
3-4pm Male and female swings with dance captain (partnering)
4-5pm Female swings with dance captain (choreography)
1-3pm Female swings with stage management (props/scenery)
4-5pm Male swings with musical director (review music)

Friday: 1-5pm 1st set of understudies and all swings called for a work-through of act one with props and scenery

An example of a typical rehearsal week (working with replacements):

When a new person comes into a show, he/she can rehearse more days per week than the rest of the company because he/she isn't performing at night. It's likely you will rehearse with him/her on a Tuesday (day after your day off) and during show-times, along with Thursday and Friday afternoons when there are no shows. If he/she is just learning one track, it usually takes him/her about a week to ten days to learn the entire show. In the second week of his/her rehearsal, you will add elements like partnering with his/her actual partners, costumes, rehearsals with other swings and understudies, and then eventually a put-in.

Tuesday:	1-4pm Replacement with musical director (learn music) 4-5pm Replacement with wardrobe (costume fitting) 7-10pm Replacement with dance captain (choreography)
Wednesday:	1-3pm Replacement with stage manger (blocking) 3-5pm Replacement with dance captain (choreography) 8-11pm Replacement watch the show
Thursday:	12 pm Replacement with shoe maker (shoe fitting) 1-5pm Replacment with dance captain (choreography) 8-11pm Replacement watch the show
Friday:	1-5pm Replacement with swings/dance captain (choreography) 8-11pm Replacement trail backstage
Saturday:	12-1pm Replacement with musical director (music) 1-5pm Replacement with dance captain (choreography) 8-11pm Replacement watch the show
Sunday:	3-6pm Replacement with dance captain (choreography)
Monday:	Day off
Tuesday:	1-3pm Replacement with musical director (music) 3-5pm Replacement with stage manager (blocking) 7-11pm Replacement watch the show
Wednesday:	1-4pm Replacement trail backstage 7pm Replacement with onstage partner (lift rehearsal) 8-11pm Replacement watch the show
Thursday:	1-5pm Replacement run-through with understudies and swings 8-11pm Replacement watch the show or trail backstage
Friday:	12pm Replacement into mic and costumes 1-5pm Full company called for Replacement's put-in 8-11pm Replacement with dance captain (for notes)
Saturday:	Replacement performs the show for the first time.

As you see, there are many versions of a weekly rehearsal. It depends on who needs to learn what. There will likely be times when you have to rehearse understudies, swings, and replacements at the same time. It's best to make a list of what you, the dance captain, need/want to do and let the stage manager schedule everything in conjunction with the other departments. Once the stage manager makes a draft schedule, he/she will likely give it to you to look over to make sure it looks right and nothing was forgotten. It takes a lot of pre-planning and organization to keep on top of everyone's needs for weekly rehearsals. This is where the lists from the swings, understudies and your own personal calendar can help. *(see p.123)*

On top of rehearsing what people need to learn, there will be other rehearsals that need to be "peppered in" during weekly rehearsals. Things like:

- Lift rehearsals with partners that are having trouble with a lift.
- New set pieces replacing old ones, actors need to try it before the show.
- A swing is going on for a show and needs to rehearse with a partner.
- An understudy needs to practise a costume change before going on.
- *Clean-up rehearsals* for the whole company (music and choreography).
- TONY award or other TV rehearsals that come up.
- Put-ins for actors before they perform the show for the first time.
- Safety/fight rehearsals with props (like guns, knives, fire).
- A swing needs to rehearse a vocal part (with a trio) before going on.
- Someone gets a new costume and his/her dresser wants to practise the quick-change.

The list is endless and will always be changing from week to week. The following week's rehearsal schedule is usually posted a day or two before everyone leaves for the day off. Even once the weekly schedule is posted, minor changes may arise as issues do. Just keep in communication with your stage manager to arrange any scheduling.

> *TIP:*
> *Talk to your stage manager about every rehearsal. Even if you need to schedule a quick lift rehearsal onstage, your stage manager will know the best time to do it. Perhaps the crew is doing their "pre-set" at a certain time and can't have you onstage. Work with the stage manager to find out what can be scheduled at what time. The crew may be able to accommodate you at the same time as their "pre-set", but they care about safety and they want the stage manager to know what's going on. The stage manager can look out for your safety during rehearsal if the crew is busy.*

Put-ins

A *put-in* is when an actor gets to rehearse with the rest of the company to simulate what it's like to perform in the show. Every show does put-ins differently. It depends on who is being put into the show. The entire company may be called to rehearse, including principals. If principals aren't called to rehearsal, the understudies will be used in the principal roles.

Every show manages put-ins differently depending on the cost involved. It is nice to have costumes, wigs, sound, orchestra, set pieces, props and automation. However, it costs a lot of money to pay crew to do that kind of rehearsal, so they are not done often. There may be elements of the above, but again, every show is different.

Make sure you communicate what you plan to do with other departments. Sometimes stage management will take care of the communication, but you will benefit when everyone is on the same page. It saves time when the music department knows what's coming next and can get the music ready. It helps if stage management knows what's coming next so they can get any props or set pieces ready. If a put-in is well planned, you should not have to wait for anything. The key is in the pre-planning!

Different types of put-ins:

There will be times when you have to organize and run a put-in. It may be done differently, depending on who is being put into the show. Here are the types of put-ins:
1. For a replacement actor (principal or chorus).
2. For an understudy or stand-by.
3. For a swing.

If a new principal actor is going into the show, it's likely the other principals will be called in to do a put-in rehearsal. If a new chorus actor is doing a put-in, the principals or the understudies will be called. If a swing is having a put-in, it's likely the understudies will do the put-in. If the swing interacts with a particular principal, then he/she might be called in privately to a separate rehearsal. The reason for this is to allow the principals to have ample rest they need to perform their role 8 times a week.

For a replacement actor:

If you are putting a replacement actor into the show, look at what *numbers* you need to go through. You will likely not have to go through the entire show. You will only practise the parts of the show where the actor is onstage or dealing with costumes backstage.

This is the first time the actor will be with the full company. The actor will likely remember the names of the actors they need to "watch for" but may not recognize everyone's faces yet. Before the put-in, or before each number, introduce the new actor to the people he/she has to be familiar with.

When the full company gets together, it becomes a "chat-fest" and people like to catch up. You don't want to kill that energy; you want to harness it and gently take control of the room. What people really want is to get it done as quickly as possible! It's a bonus to finish before the allotted time. They really want someone to take charge and not waste their time. The best way to start is with a brief speech to the company. The stage manager may also want to start the rehearsal with a brief speech. If so, you can add on to it after so the company knows you are also in control. Introduce the new member, thank the company for coming and tell them how the rehearsal will be run.

Here's an example of a brief speech to start the put-in:

> *"Hey guys! I want to introduce you to the newest member of our family, Callie! (Everyone will likely cheer). This is the first time she is onstage with the full company, so she will be looking for faces that belong to the names she learned in rehearsals. Feel free to help her out and introduce yourself as we get to that number. She has been working really hard and we want to make sure we get through everything efficiently today so she feels comfortable going on tonight. (again cheers) I am going to thank you in advance for your patience and focus as we go through rehearsal today. I know it's easy to chat with friends in rehearsal, but I may have to remind you to keep the chatter down so Callie can hear what she needs. It's also hard for me to talk over many voices so please don't take offense when I say, and I will say, 'quiet please'. Before we run the numbers, we will space through it and talk through*

any company notes while Callie talks through costume changes. This gives us a chance to do the notes 'on their feet' so we can be efficient and avoid a company note session. So thanks for your cooperation and let's do it! (with a big smile) We will start with...."

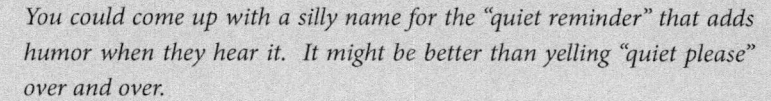

> **TIP:**
> *You could come up with a silly name for the "quiet reminder" that adds humor when they hear it. It might be better than yelling "quiet please" over and over.*

You will likely want to *walk through* or *space through* a number before you run it with music in real time. This means that you would start at the beginning of the number and talk through the positions or choreography without music, just counts. This allows the actor to get his/her bearings with the full cast onstage. This is when you can start and stop the rehearsal if there are problems. You want to make sure the new actor feels completely comfortable in the number before you run the number with music. Have the paper where you notated the counting of the music close by so you can reference it if needed. Once you have completed the walk through, ask the actor if he/she feels comfortable to run the number now. You can also ask the company if there were any things you need to go over again. Once everyone says they are okay, you can run the number with music.

You can give the company any choreographic, acting and music notes before you space the number. Or, you can do it between spacing the number and running the number. Some notes are better given before the company has to space or run a number, so they can practise the note a few times. Some notes can be done while the new actor is dealing with wardrobe and hair departments.

For an understudy or stand-by:

An understudy is usually a chorus person in the show performing his/her own track in the show every night. They do not get the chance to watch what the principal is doing, who they cover. They may be *swung out* one show to watch or trail backstage, but that would not give enough information for them to step onstage and perform the role. They would likely need a put-in with the company and practise costume and wig changes too.

A stand-by will have ample time to watch the show or trail but it doesn't substitute for being on the stage with the company around you. The stand-by will likely need a put-in too. Try and do this as soon as possible because he or she will be expected to perform a role before the understudy is asked. A stand-by is usually only hired for a star or one of the leading roles. You want to make sure he or she is very comfortable to perform and "carry the show".

For a swing:

If it's the first time a swing is going on, then you would likely have a more extensive put-in with the company, if the situation allows. If a swing has already performed in one track, then you will likely only have to put him/her into a few numbers. Depending on how much you have to put the swing into and how long it will take, you can have the company come in early before a show. This way the company avoids having to come in for a separate afternoon rehearsal. They usually prefer this. The main priority is the swing though, so make sure you have a conversation with the swing to find out what he/she wants to go through with the company. Once you know, you can decide how long it will take and schedule accordingly.

We will talk about how to "schedule" a put-in in the following chapter. It takes a decent amount of forethought and organization to plan a put-in and have it run efficiently. It's all in the pre-planning. The more work you do in the planning, the quicker and more efficient the put-in rehearsal will be. If you can incorporate clean-up notes as well when you put the new company member in, it will feel productive for the whole company. The company will appreciate not being called in for a separate clean-up rehearsal.

> TIP:
> You don't always have the luxury of scheduling a put-in before a swing has to go on. If you can incorporate a swing into a track little by little in other actors' put-ins or weekly rehearsals, do so. That way, he or she has more time onstage with the company before performing in front of an audience.

Here is a typical day for a put-in:

1. Make sure all departments know what to expect in the put-in. This can be done with a printed list of what needs to be done and given to all department heads (musical director, wardrobe supervisor or dresser, sound, lighting, props, carpenters, stage manager, dance captain)
2. The replacement actor will get dressed in wigs, costume and mic.
3. The rest of the company will put on mics. (no wigs or costumes)
4. Introduce the new company member and set the tone for a happy, yet efficient, put-in with a brief speech to officially start the put-in.
5. Do the show in "chunks", starting and stopping as needed.
6. If time permits, give the company notes before *spacing* numbers. Check in with other departments (music and stage management) to see if they want to give any notes.
7. *Space/Walk through* (without music) parts of the numbers that are complicated.
8. Talk through and practise any partnering lifts (in costume) that the actor will do in each section.
9. Run the section with costume and music. Announce to everyone (the company, music department and wardrobe) where you will start from and where you will finish, making sure you include the costume change.
10. Have someone notify you when the costume change is over so you can stop the music.
11. Continue onto the next section.

TIP:
If the principals are not called to a put-in, make sure everyone knows who is filling in the gaps. The understudies and swings need to know in advance what they will be doing in each number. It saves time in the put-in and alleviates stress by giving people advanced notice.

It's not a good idea just to *run through* a number to music without spacing it first, unless the actor says he/she doesn't need it. If it's a really simple or short number, then sometimes you can run through it. As long as you have done ample rehearsal previously with the actor, this may allow you to run a number without spacing first.

Here is an example of a put-in schedule posted for the company:

Callie and Matt Put-in

1. **"Requiem"** through **"Quartet"**

2. **"BA"** through **"Art of Possible"**

3. **"Charity"** (*I don't always rush in*) through **"Another Suitcase"**.

4. **"Peron's Latest Flame"** through **"A New Argentina"**

INTERMISSION

5. **"Balcony"** (*skipping Don't Cry*) through **"The Chorus Girl Hasn't Learned"**

6. **"Money"** through **"Santa Evita"**

7. **"She's a Diamond"**

8. **"Montage"** (*bed entrance*) through **"Bows"**

We are not running:
Junin
the beginning of Charity Concert
Eva singing Don't Cry For Me on Balcony
The Waltz
You must love me
Dice are Rolling
Eva's final Broadcast

You will likely post something for the company that is simple to read and easy to understand. (Stage management posts it for you.) However, you may want to have your own version of the put-in so you know what you want to do and who will be doing what. On the next page, you will find a version of the same put-in, for the dance captain.

Callie and Matt Put-in (Dance Captain copy)

1. Space "**Requiem/M. Tango**" then run into "**end of "Quartet"**" for QC
   Jennie (Constantine) will partner with Erica. Cut Laurel for put-in only.

2. Space "BA/Lovers" then run "**BA to end of Art of Possible**" for crossover/QC
   BA:
   Alternate spacing for Jennie (Constantine/Colin) and MJ (Constantine entering later). Also Laurel will be cut for put-in.
   Lovers:
   Cut Johnny. Johnny does Colin.
   Art of the Possible:
   Matt does Bradley for put-in only.

3. Space Charity concert (middle). Run "**Charity**" to end of "**Another Suitcase**".
   Cut Colin in Charity and Constantine in Another suitcase.

4. Space "**Peron's Flame**" and "**New Argentina**" then run.
   No Bradley or Laurel for put-in only. (Crew grabs props)

5. Space "**Balcony, High Flying, Rainbow High, Rainbow Tour**" then run to end of "**The Chorus Girl Hasn't Learned**" (until they are changed).
   Balcony/High Flying:
   Cut Laurel for put-in only.
   Rainbow High/Tour:
   Cut Laurel and Bradley for put-in only.

6. Space "**Money**" and "**Santa Evita**" then run
   Jennie does Laurel for Put-in only.

7. Space "**She's a Diamond**" then run
   Colin (Johnny)   Daniel (Jason)   Constantine (MJ)

8. Space "**Montage**", "**Lament**" and "**Bows**" then run
   Cut Bradley and Laurel for put-in only.

(We are not running "Junin'", the beginning of "Charity Concert", "The Waltz", "You must love me", "Dice are Rolling")

In the above example, you can see more detail. This helps the dance captain run the rehearsal efficiently. You know exactly where to start and stop in the music. You know who will be stepping in to what roles to help the put-in run smoothly. By pre-planning, you eliminate the time it takes to figure these things out.

Brush-up rehearsals

A *brush-up* rehearsal is when the full company or just the full chorus is called to rehearse notes for the show. There are times when a show needs a *clean up* of choreography or music. This usually happens in longer running shows. A brush-up rehearsal can be called anytime, as long as it is part of the allowable weekly rehearsal hours. A dance captain may feel that there are too many notes to give to the company now and it warrants getting everyone together in the same room to clean up the choreography. It also is a good idea to get the full company back in a rehearsal studio, in front of mirrors, to rehearse choreography. Sometimes, the actors just need to see what they are doing compared to the rest of the company. That way you can point out differences and corrections in a way they can identify. It's hard for a performing actor to see what his/her fellow actors are doing onstage.

> *TIP:*
> *Most companies complain about being called for a brush-up rehearsal. It's another day they have to give up to come to the theatre. They already come in for put-ins. If you can, try to incorporate the full company notes into the put-ins instead.*

Lift rehearsals

There will likely be a lot of lift rehearsals in a musical. A dance captain is responsible for running those rehearsals and making sure everyone is safe. The best way to handle a lift rehearsal is to talk through the lift first! There is a difference between doing a lift rehearsal with actors who have never done the lift before and those who have. If an actor has never done the lift before, you really have to teach him or her how to do it first.

When you talk through a lift for the first time, you explain the mechanics of the lift from all aspects. This can include: hand grips, timing, what your body is doing, what the legs and arms do, how to help your partner, or what to avoid.

Teaching a lift for the first time:

If you were going to teach a simple "Juliet lift" like the picture below, you would start by teaching the lift's mechanics with the guy and then with the girl.

Here is an example of how to teach the mechanics of a lift:

Starting with the guy: (It doesn't matter who you start with)
"She will run to you from the front. Keep your hips facing her to make sure your body is square, avoiding uneven pressure on your lower back. The palms of your hands will squeeze in around her hips and waist area. You will be lifting her whole body weight from her waist/hips. To help you lift her weight, you want to use your strongest muscles, which are your thighs, along with help from your

biceps and the timing of her jump. Just before you "toss her in the air", you want to plié (bend your knees) deep enough so you use all of your thigh strength. At the same time, it's good to keep your elbows in to your body so you engage your biceps and lats. You will "feel" the timing of her jump. She will plié and as she is coming up from her plié, you help her jump by quickly and forcefully using your thighs to stand up more, squeezing your palms in as you extend your arms over your head. When she is at the height of her jump, you will let go and wrap your forearms around the back of her thighs. The most ideal place to grab is lower on the hamstring, above the knees, so she remains nice and high in the lift. If you can reach, you can grab your forearms or elbows with your opposite hands. (show him) Keep your head straight forward and don't look to the side. This will prevent any straining of your neck."

"What to be mindful of:
- If you keep your elbows out, there is more pressure on your wrists and your biceps can't help as much.
- Avoid grabbing the girl too high (under the ribs) or digging your thumbs in too tightly. Use the squeezing pressure of your palms towards each other, versus the digging in of your thumbs. This will avoid bruising of her ribs or body. If you grab too high, then she's basically hanging her whole weight off her ribs and your thumbs. It may accidentally happen once in a while, but if consistently done like this, you could cause injury to her ribs and your thumbs.
- The final thing you want to remember is when you plié, don't stick your bum way out and create a 'sway back'. This will put all her body weight into your lower back. You want to keep your back straight when you plié and keep her weight in your thighs."

If you are a female dance captain, you can try it with the male dancer first before he does it with his partner. This way you can tell what is happening. You can give praise and give corrections.

To the girl:
"You are going to run to him from the front. He is looking for your hips so try to keep them straight towards him. You will start the jump in "5th position" or "3rd position" with your left foot in front (show her). This allows you to use both legs during the jump. You will plié right before the jump and put your hands on his shoulders.

Your last step before the "jump prep" will be on your right foot and it will be right in front of him, as far away as it feels comfortable for you. (You can practise the run, last step is the R foot, then into a 3rd position in plié with the left foot in front. After that is mastered, you can add an unassisted jump after the plié so she gets used to jumping.) This allows you to find your body weight and not rely on the guy to do everything. Once you can jump in the air, the guy will just help you go higher. You will use your legs and arms to help you. Once your hands are on his shoulders, you can use them to push down as you go up. This will help take some of your body weight on his shoulders. When you are at the top, you will reach your arms in the air overhead in 5th position (show her)."

"What to be mindful of:
- Keep your arms out of the way as you run to him so he has a clear path to grip you.
- You don't have to plié too much or your knees may hit his legs. Just plié a little so he knows the timing of when you are ready to jump.
- When you plié and jump in the air, you want to keep your body straight and not arch. You can do this by not sticking your bum out on the plié or throwing your upper body back in the air. You may think it helps him, but it doesn't. It just throws the momentum back from you and forward for him. It's best to stay straight.
- Do not lean forward when you plié. If you lean forward to look down, you could hit heads with your partner right before the lift."

    Praise is always good, especially if someone is not used to doing lifts. What may come naturally to dancers, can seem like information overload to others. Practice makes perfect. If they are uncomfortable or self-conscious, keep asking questions. You want to know their fears and hesitations versus shoving more words at them. You want to make sure they are clear. There will be moments when an actor does not understand and there will be moments when they just need to take a chance to get over their fears. Be aware and sensitive to those differences. Truly encourage the actor that he or she can do it, without being patronizing. Never show frustration because that doesn't help anyone. Let them know that they can expect the lift to get better and better.

Running a lift rehearsal with actors who know the lift:

There will be times when a swing, understudy or stand-by has to rehearse a lift before doing the show. This is done for safety reasons. They already know the lift but need to be reminded of the timing and practise it without an audience. It's best to talk through the timing of the lift as well as the hand grips and what each actor can expect. Most often this is done on the stage before a show or during intermission. There will be no orchestra or music capabilities so you will have to count the choreography when you run the rehearsal

Here's an example of how to talk through a pre-show lift rehearsal:

> "You start with the left foot on this section. Just a reminder (to the guys), Christina likes your hands lower on her back because of the height difference. We are going to talk through it without the lift. Just walk through the counts. We will take it from 'this' section until the end of 8 counts after the lift." Then you count the choreography. At the end of the walk-through, you can ask if they are ready to do the lift. Somebody might say something they forgot to mention last time they did the lift. Christina may ask about a timing reminder.

> *TIP:*
> *It's very important to know the proper counting of the music for any rehearsal where you won't have music to accompany you. You can easily derail and frustrate the actors if you are counting the music and choreography incorrectly!*

Safety rehearsals

Safety rehearsals are done for things that are more "stunt" factor than choreography. Most of the time a *fight captain* is hired to maintain and run these rehearsals. Examples include: fight sequences, the use of guns or knives, fire effects, and so on. If a show has these type of effects, it's likely that they will schedule a *fight call* or *safety call* before every show or at least once a day on a double show day. You are not required to be at these calls if you are not the fight captain. However, there may be some aspects that cross over to choreography and then you may be asked by stage management to be there to observe.

Partnering rehearsals

There may be a time when you come across two actors who have trouble working together. There are many reasons why they might not get along. The responsibility that comes with being their dance captain is you have to find a way to mediate and get the job done.

When one partner blames the other for not being a good partner:

Just because one actor claims the other is a bad partner, does not mean it's true. It might mean they aren't good partners for each other. One actor might need certain things from the other that he/she is not getting. Most likely both actors want the show to be good. They want to look good doing the lift and that is where their frustrations stem from. Use that as a launching point for a private discussion with each of them. It doesn't matter who you talk to first.

- Find out what she believes to be the problem.
- Find out what she thinks he could do to help her.
- Guide the conversation to a more compassionate level by saying something like, "I know he really wants to make you look good, and he's feeling like he can't do anything right. He's starting to second guess his abilities, and he's never felt like that before."
- Suggest, "Perhaps he can work on those feelings, but you have the power to help him or crush his spirit. No one wants to feel inadequate and I really want the two of you to find resolution with all of this. Wouldn't it be great to get to a point where you enjoyed each other versus dreading the moment? Negative feelings set you up for failure, but I have faith we can turn this situation around!"
- Ask her if there is anything she can do to help the situation as we work together to find a solution.
- Tell her that you are going to use her suggestions as you work one-on-one with her partner, and then find a time when the two of them can try the lifts with each other.

This conversation may help her realize she could be co-creating the negativity and it's not just the partner causing the problem. It will likely help her be more compassionate and willing to work with him during the next rehearsal. It may not fix the technical problems of partnering, but attitude is most of it! There are plenty of partners who don't do things perfectly every night, but they accept it as part of the process because they like each other.

> *TIP:*
> *Getting partners to rehearse separately allows them the freedom to talk about what is not going well, without worrying about hurting the other partner's feelings. A dance captain should be the buffer and help each partner sort through it. There should not be a "blame game" in front of each other. It's a partnership.*

Then you can go to the guy and ask him what the problem is.
- Find out what he thinks she could do to help him.
- Guide him to a compassionate level and say, "She only wants the best for you two and her frustrations come out of that. She feels badly about how she has reacted and wants to find a way to make you feel confident about taking charge in the lifts".
- Encourage his confidence because all girls respect a confident partner, especially if she is a strong woman. Tell him that he doesn't always have to sit quietly and let her complain. He can also be vocal about what he needs from her. Encourage him to communicate the next time they are doing a lift rehearsal, so she knows he's not a "push-over".
- Ask him if there is anything he can do to help the situation.
- Tell him you would like to work on the lifts separately (with you) so he feels free to communicate what he feels is working and what is not.
- Then once you have done that, you can get them together to rehearse. Try to pick a convenient time for both, where both have input into when they will rehearse. This makes sure there is no added resentment or "fuel to the fire" about having to come in extra to rehearse lifts with a partner you find difficult to work with.

"Things can and do turn around. I pride myself in being able to partner anyone and I love partnering all different types. But, I had a partner in one show I 'hated' to work with. I was willing to try anything. He disliked the choreographer and never wanted to try anything the choreographer asked. We were both out for our own interests and in turn, hurt each other and ourselves by not getting along. We got to know each other on a personal level, outside of the show, over the next year. Our trust built and so did the fun. By the end of the run, I felt like he was trying harder and I loved dancing with him. He ended up being my favorite dance partner. "   - Anonymous

CHAPTER 11

Scheduling

You will work with the stage managers to help create a rehearsal schedule for the next week. Other departments will submit a list of what they want to accomplish. Stage management will gather the notes to make one weekly schedule incorporating everyone's wishes. There may not be enough time to accomplish everything, so it's important to know what your priorities are.

Keep a "running list"

In order to schedule properly, you have to have an idea of what to schedule. It's good to keep a "running list" of **everything** you need to do. You also need an idea of the priority for what needs to get done.

Some things to keep in mind as you make your overall running list:

- Are the understudies ready to go on? If not, what do they need to learn or rehearse?
- Are the swings ready to go on for all their tracks? If not, what do they need to learn or rehearse?
- Are there any vacations or personal days coming up? Is the understudy or swing prepared to go on for that track or role?
- Is there anything that takes more time to teach and perfect, such as partnering lifts, acrobatics, or other effects?
- Are there replacement cast members who need to be taught?

Start with making a list of everything you need to accomplish. Keep a running list of things you need to do and include what people tell you they need.

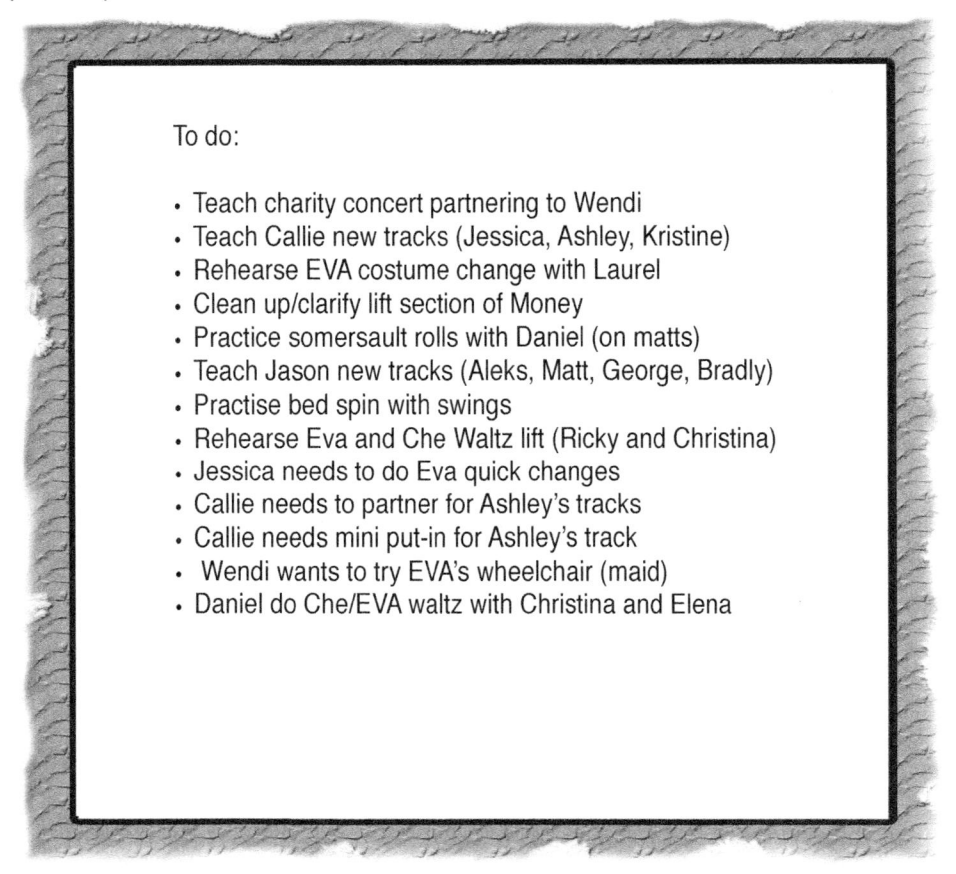

To do:

- Teach charity concert partnering to Wendi
- Teach Callie new tracks (Jessica, Ashley, Kristine)
- Rehearse EVA costume change with Laurel
- Clean up/clarify lift section of Money
- Practice somersault rolls with Daniel (on matts)
- Teach Jason new tracks (Aleks, Matt, George, Bradly)
- Practise bed spin with swings
- Rehearse Eva and Che Waltz lift (Ricky and Christina)
- Jessica needs to do Eva quick changes
- Callie needs to partner for Ashley's tracks
- Callie needs mini put-in for Ashley's track
- Wendi wants to try EVA's wheelchair (maid)
- Daniel do Che/EVA waltz with Christina and Elena

How to Make a Weekly Schedule

You won't really be involved in planning the weekly schedule during rehearsals and tech. Once the show is open and you are responsible for teaching, then you will be more involved in scheduling. Once you have an overall idea of what you need to do, then you can look at your deadlines and prioritize what you need to accomplish the following week.

Once you prioritize what needs to be done, calculate how long each of those things will take and schedule accordingly. Also look at the people involved to rehearse each item and see if you can group it so people aren't waiting around. It is helpful to make your own "dance captain calendar" to ensure you get what you need done. This would include vacations, replacements, lifts to teach, and so forth. This will allow you to "work backwards" and make sure you have scheduled ample time to do everything by certain dates.

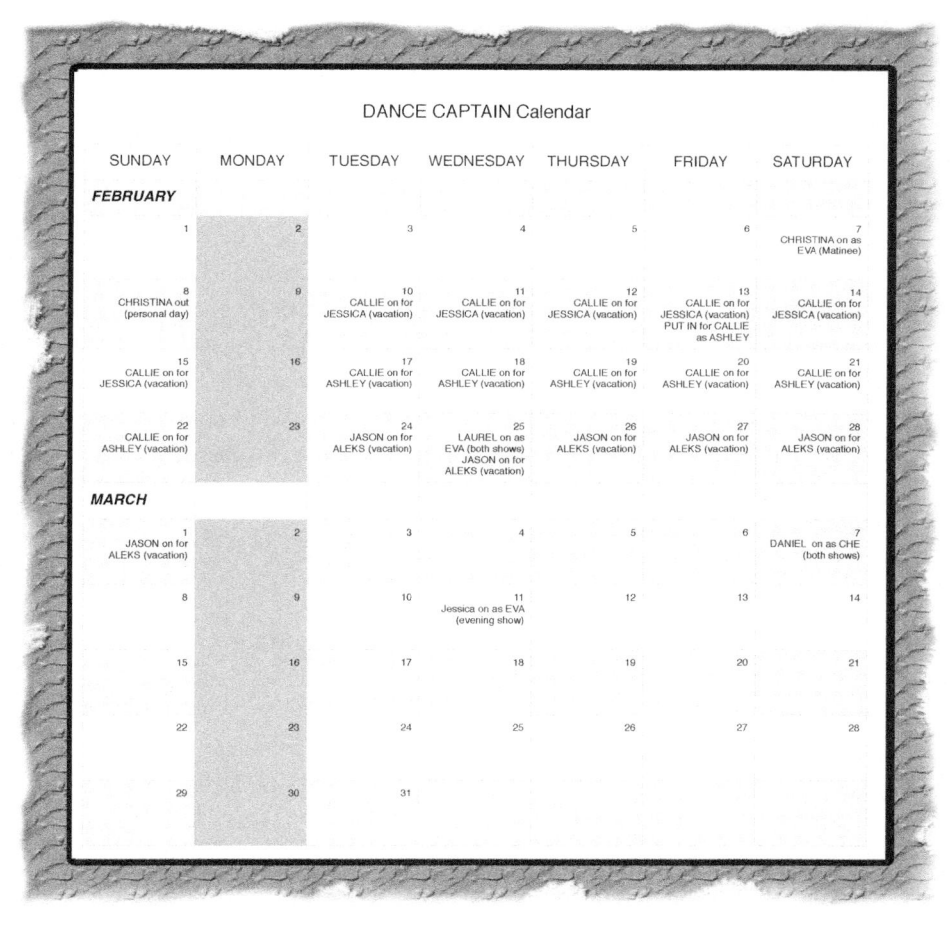

DANCE CAPTAIN Calendar

FEBRUARY

SUNDAY	MONDAY	TUESDAY	WEDNESDAY	THURSDAY	FRIDAY	SATURDAY
1	2	3	4	5	6	7 CHRISTINA on as EVA (Matinee)
8 CHRISTINA out (personal day)	9	10 CALLIE on for JESSICA (vacation)	11 CALLIE on for JESSICA (vacation)	12 CALLIE on for JESSICA (vacation)	13 CALLIE on for JESSICA (vacation) PUT IN for CALLIE as ASHLEY	14 CALLIE on for JESSICA (vacation)
15 CALLIE on for JESSICA (vacation)	16	17 CALLIE on for ASHLEY (vacation)	18 CALLIE on for ASHLEY (vacation)	19 CALLIE on for ASHLEY (vacation)	20 CALLIE on for ASHLEY (vacation)	21 CALLIE on for ASHLEY (vacation)
22 CALLIE on for ASHLEY (vacation)	23	24 JASON on for ALEKS (vacation)	25 LAUREL on as EVA (both shows) JASON on for ALEKS (vacation)	26 JASON on for ALEKS (vacation)	27 JASON on for ALEKS (vacation)	28 JASON on for ALEKS (vacation)

MARCH

SUNDAY	MONDAY	TUESDAY	WEDNESDAY	THURSDAY	FRIDAY	SATURDAY
1 JASON on for ALEKS (vacation)	2	3	4	5	6	7 DANIEL on as CHE (both shows)
8	9	10	11 Jessica on as EVA (evening show)	12	13	14
15	16	17	18	19	20	21
22	23	24	25	26	27	28
29	30	31				

By looking at your own calendar, you can see what needs to be done quickly and what can wait. Here are some things to take note of in the example above:

- I can see that Christina will be on for EVA Feb 7th. That means I have to schedule the waltz rehearsal with Ricky and Christina by then. It will take about 15 minutes so I can likely schedule it on that day, before the show starts. The skirt seems to be an issue so I will also request that

she gets to put on her dress and heels for that rehearsal. You don't have to worry about talking to wardrobe directly. You just make the request to stage management and they will arrange it.
- I can also see that Jessica is on vacation soon, so Callie, the vacation swing, needs to learn her track the week before. Then she will also need a mini put-in that Friday for Jessica's track. The mini put-in will involve most of the chorus.
- I look to see if I can do company clean up notes to make the most of my time with the company. I can clean up and clarify the lift section of "Money". Perhaps the music department will also have company notes they want to do.
- Christina has a personal day on Feb 8th. She is the standby for the lead role, EVA. If the woman who regularly plays EVA gets sick, then an understudy will go on. That means I should make sure Jessica is ready to go on and has practised her quick changes before being thrown on. We can find 20 minutes before a show to do those this week.
- I need access to the bed to rehearse the swings with the tricky bed move. The crew preset happens before the show so perhaps we can have 10 minutes with the bed onstage while the crew continue to preset. If not, we will have access to the bed during the put-in and just have to schedule time for the swings to do what they need to do.

Now you can schedule the "must do's" first and then add the other things around it. Some things will have to wait until the following week or later.

Make a list of what you want to do for stage management, and they will put it into a weekly schedule to send out to the company. *Your* list would look something like this:

Dance Captain's "to-do" list

- Wednesday: Have Jess do her EVA quick changes(20 mins).
- Thursday: Rehearse Callie (finish Jessica's track)
- Friday: Mini put-in with cast (2 hrs), bring in Callie's partners 30 mins before the full company to work with her, swings rehearse with the bed for (10 mins); clean up and clarifty the lift section of Money because the whole chorus is called in already (take 15 minutes in the put-in)
- Saturday (mat): Rehearse Eva lift onstage (15 mins) with Christina and Ricky (in costume)
- Rehearse the somersault with Daniel three times this week.

Stage management will take your information and combine it with other departments' lists. Then you will likely be sent a draft copy. Each department will look over the draft copy to see if changes need to be made. Once all departments have "okayed" the schedule, it will be sent out.

> *TIP:*
> *Don't forget about mandatory union breaks! The actors and musicians need a 5 minute break every hour. In lieu of breaking every hour, you may rehearse for 1hr and 20 minutes before taking a 10 minute break. You don't want to get stuck scheduling something you needed half an hour for, but you have to stop after 20 minutes because of a break.*

Here is an example of a weekly rehearsal schedule:

EVITA REHEARSAL SCHEDULE - WEEK OF Feb 1-7
SUBJECT TO CHANGE

Tuesday, February 3

| 7:00-7:15p | Roll rehearsal: D.Torres w/J.Ford |

Wednesday, February 4

1:30-5:00p	C.Carter (Jessica track) w/J.Ford @ Pearl studios
7:00-7:20p	J.Patty (EVA quick changes) with costumes on deck
7:20-7:30p	B.A.Lifts: C.DeCicco, M.von Essen, A. Pevec, N. Kenkel, C. Germanacos, J. Stellard, A. Stoll w/M.Wall onstage

Thursday, February 5

| 1:00-5:00p | C.Carter (Jessica track) w/J.Ford onstage |
| 7:00-7:15p | Roll rehearsal: D.Torres w/J.Ford |

Friday, February 6

1:00-1:30p	C.Carter (Jessica track) w/J.Ford onstage
1:30-2:00p	ADD: A.Pevec, D.Torres, J.Stellard, partnering with Callie
2:00-4:30p	ADD: full ensemble (including swings) put-in for Callie onstage ("BA, Peron's Flame", "Money") Clean and clarify "money" bed rehearsal for swings
4:30-5:00p	FULL ENSEMBLE: Vocal "brush up" w/K.Blodgette onstage

Saturday, February 7

| 2:10-2:30p | R.Martin and C. DeCicco (EVA) waltz reh w/J.Ford onstage with dress |
| 7:00-7:15p | Roll rehearsal: D.Torres w/J.Ford |

How to Schedule a Put-in

The trick to scheduling a put-in is calculating how long everything will take. Consider the following: How much of it do you have to mark through first without music? How much time will it take to deal with costumes? What can you do between numbers while he/she is dealing with costumes? How much time will it take for the set up of each section? Who will be doing what in each number? Is it a good idea to have some of the understudies or swings practise parts?

The main focus is always giving the actor, who's being put-in, a chance to do everything onstage with everyone, and the notes and clean up should just be "fillers" to make the most of the company's time.

> *TIP:*
> *Don't forget to account for the time it takes the crew to preset and do the intermission change-over for the put-in. Could you be working on other things like partnering, company notes, vocal notes or costume changes tomake use of that time?*

1. Start by making a list of all the numbers the replacement is in.
2. Figure out where the actor needs to start in a number and where you will end, including costume changes. (This can be multiple numbers.)
3. Figure out what sections of the number need to be spaced without music before you run it to music with the company.
4. Estimate how long it will take to do what you need to for the actor during the put-in.
5. Be mindful of when the actor has quick changes and when you will need to run the music continuously to make sure he/she makes it.
6. Figure out which costume changes are not quick changes. You are able to stop the music once the actor leaves the stage and address some of your *clean up notes* with the full company while the actor changes.
7. Make a list of "clean up notes" that you can address during rehearsal time because it's rare to get the full company called in for rehearsal. Date the document so you know when you did it.
8. Assign who will do what in each number, to make sure the actor has the people he/she needs to interact with during the put-in.

Here is an example of a put-in schedule:

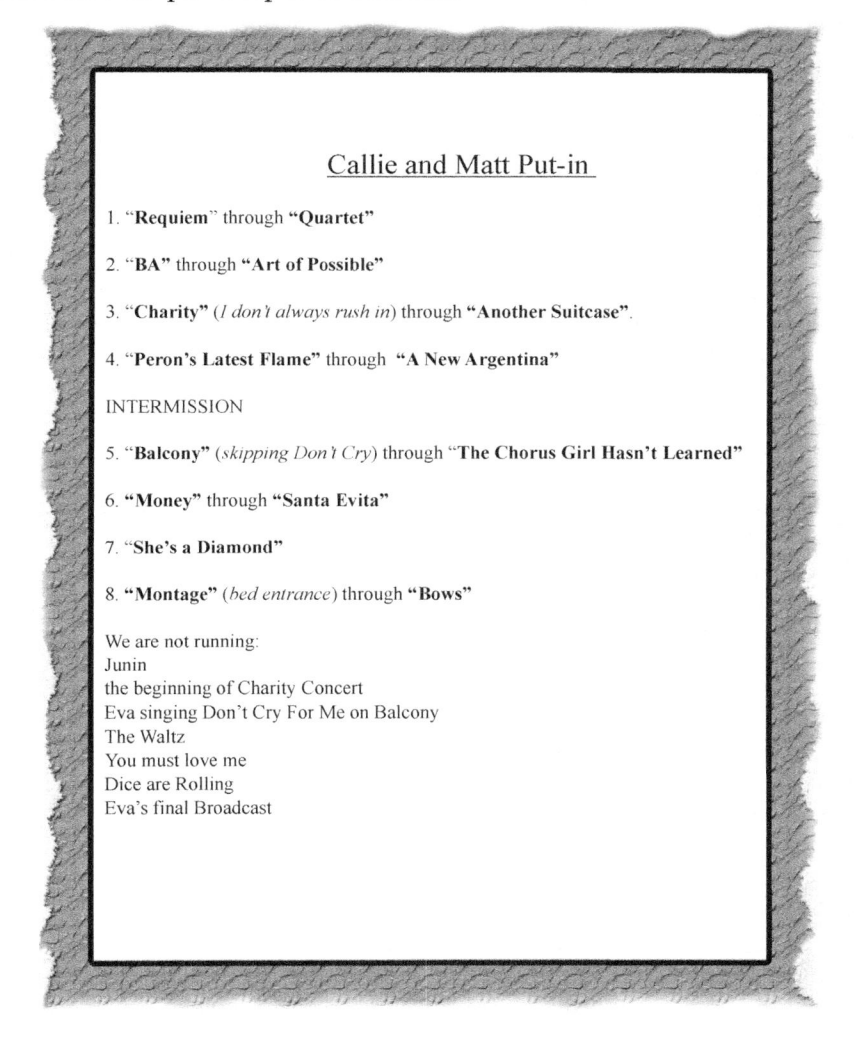

> ### Callie and Matt Put-in
>
> 1. **"Requiem"** through **"Quartet"**
>
> 2. **"BA"** through **"Art of Possible"**
>
> 3. **"Charity"** (*I don't always rush in*) through **"Another Suitcase"**.
>
> 4. **"Peron's Latest Flame"** through **"A New Argentina"**
>
> INTERMISSION
>
> 5. **"Balcony"** (*skipping Don't Cry*) through **"The Chorus Girl Hasn't Learned"**
>
> 6. **"Money"** through **"Santa Evita"**
>
> 7. **"She's a Diamond"**
>
> 8. **"Montage"** (*bed entrance*) through **"Bows"**
>
> We are not running:
> Junin
> the beginning of Charity Concert
> Eva singing Don't Cry For Me on Balcony
> The Waltz
> You must love me
> Dice are Rolling
> Eva's final Broadcast

As we explained in the previous chapter, a dance captain may want to write more detailed things he/she needs to assist in running the rehearsal. Things, such as who will be doing what roles, where you want to stop and start, when the quick changes happen, when you want to space a number before running it. This **detailed** *put-in schedule* will only be for you. You will likely want to make another put-in schedule (like the example above) to post for the company with less information, to make it easier to read. Just make sure swings and understudies know what they are doing during the put-in.

How to Schedule Lift Rehearsals

1) Start by making a list of the lifts you need to do in the rehearsal.
2) Does everyone already know the lift? Do you just need practise?
3) Do you have to teach a new person the mechanics of the lift?
4) Estimate how much time it will take.
5) Write down who is involved in each lift.
6) Can you schedule it in such a way that it has the fewest people sitting around waiting?

List of all the lifts needing to be done:

- Matt and Christina parter (BA)
- Matt and boys (Alex, Aleks, Johnny, Nick) with Christina (BA lifts)
- Callie and Alex (Charity concert, Money and Montage lifts)
- Matt and Little Girl (shoulder lift)
- Matt and Brad (soldier fight)

Things to take into consideration:

- The "Little Girl" is only in one lift so bring her in last.
- There are two dance captains so we could be working on lifts at the same time.
- Brad is only needed for one fight so bring him in later.
- Callie has never done the lifts with her partner Alex and may need some time getting used to him.
- Alex is needed by Matt and Callie for rehearsal.

LIFT SCHEDULE

1:00pm	Matt, Christina, Alex, Aleks, Johnny, Nick w/M.Wall (BA Lifts)
1:10pm	Callie and Alex w/J.Ford (Charity concert, Money and Montage lifts)
1:20pm	add Little Girl w/M.Wall (shoulder sit)
1:25pm	add Brad w/M.Wall (soldier fight)
1:30pm	start put-in

Note: Callie and Matt will be doing these lift rehearsals in their costumes to get used to it and because it's right before the start of the put-in. They will be the only two in costume.

CHAPTER 12

Running Auditions

There will likely be times when you have to run auditions. Equity requires Broadway shows to hold chorus calls every six months, whether a replacement is needed or not. These are called *Equity Required Chorus Calls*. Any member of Equity, with or without an agent, can sign up to audition. You will audition males for half the day and females for the other half of the day. You could have between 50-300 of each gender show up to audition. There will also be non-equity performers who come, hoping to audition.

The equity monitor will consult with you (or the person running the dance audition) as to the audition specifics. You should be prepared to answer these questions:

- How many actors will be in each group?
- What should they wear on their feet? (heels, flats, taps, pointe shoes)
- How long will the combination be?
- Once they have learned it, they will do it for you in small groups. How many people will you have in each group? How many times will you run each group?
- Will you see the non-Equity performers?
- Is there more than one combination and when will you call people back for it?

The number of actors in each group will be determined by the room size, the choreography and how many people show up to audition. You have to think about the choreography and how many people you could have in the room dancing safely beside one another. You also have to think about how long the combination is and how you can see as many actors as possible. For example, you may have 120 Equity females show up and 90 non-Equity. You may think you can fit up to 30 people in the room, and you have 4 hours to get through dancing and singing the girls.

It would take 4 groups of 30 to get through the Equity girls and 3 groups to get through the non-equity. Let's assume you teach them the combination in 25 minutes and see them in groups of 3. If you only let them perform once, then you will have to run the audition combo 10 times to see each group of 30. If you wanted to give them two chances, you have to run the audition combo 20 times. This means each group would likely take about 45 minutes to get through.

There may be choices you have to make, depending on what is most important to you. Is it more important to see as many people as possible or to see the actors' technique. You can make a choice to cut down the combination for the non-equity actors. You could run the combination one time when they perform. You could decide not to see non-equity this time, if there are too many Equity actors who show up.

Just be prepared to teach and run the combination many times that day! It is hard to keep the same stamina throughout the day. Even though you have done it 100 times that day, each group that comes in is seeing you for the first time. Keep hydrated and stretched throughout the day to protect your body. You will likely have to go to the show that night as well. It's a long day!

What you will do with each group during the audition:

- Teach the combination to the group.
- Answer any questions the actors may have.
- Split the group up if they need more space to practise the dance.
- See them in smaller groups of 2-5 people at a time.
- Make notes on the actors and decide if you want to see more of them.
- Give the information to the casting director so he or she can announce the names of those who will stay or come back later to dance/sing.

The Audition Combination

The next group will come in and you repeat the process. At the end of all the groups, you will either dance them more or they will sing for the musical director.

The Audition Combination

Someone will have to create an audition combination to make sure you see everything you need from the actors auditioning. It can be a piece of choreography from the show. More often, it's a cut version of one or more pieces of the show's choreography. This allows you to see more technical requirements in a short time.

> EVITA
> AUDITION COMBO
> 1) "What's new Buenos Aires"
>   walk around 14, 15, 16
> 2) "You're a tramp, you're a treat"
>   (x R point L) and back up
> 3) Step L, R arm up, turn (3)
>   hold (4) developé R (5,6)
>   walk (7, 8 &)
> 4) "Hello" step w/ double chainé
>   after chin
> 5) step R, x L, "Coin flick" (3)
>   step R, L (4 &)
> 6) "Stand back" choreo
>   walk around 1 2 3 4 &
> 7) "Tramp/Treat" other way
>   (x L point R)
> 8) back up then do step at end
>   into kicks at the end
> 9) step L (1) kick R (2) envelopé (3)
>   step R (4) step L (5) kick (6)
>   envelopé (&) step R (7)

You may decide to add a high kick or a triple pirouette in the audition combo even though it is not part of the show's original choreography. You would do this to see the actor's flexibility and technique for turns that is needed in other parts of the show. For example, the audition combination for EVITA had a double chainé instead of a single and a difficult layout kick was added from another part of the show.

> *TIP:*
> *It's important to remember the combination the next time you run auditions. It may not happen for months, so it's a good idea to write it down!*

It's also a good idea to know the music and what is different about the music that will be used for the audition versus the show. You will likely have a different piano player for each audition and you have to explain what the "cuts" in the music are, if they are not clearly marked. If you do not read music, then ask your musical director to help put markings and an explanation on a copy of the music you will use. Keep a copy with you to give to the piano player in case someone forgets it. It's usually the job of the casting director to bring the music and hire the pianist. If they forget to bring the music, you are the one stuck running the audition though. It's always better to be prepared.

If you are auditioning for a specific replacement, keep in mind his or her track in the show. Are there specialties and lifts you need to try before making a decision about hiring someone new? For instance, there are plenty of terrific dancers who can't partner well and you want to make sure you cover everything in the audition.

CHAPTER 13

What to Expect When Actors Call Out

Daily "in/out" Sheet

When you get to the theatre, you will see the *daily in/out sheet*.

EVITA
DAILY IN/OUT

DATE	Friday 7/20/12		Evening
OUT	IN		NOTES
R. Martin	D. Torres		As Che
	M. Wall		On for Torres
	M. Simpson-Ernst		As child
E. Mansfield	J. Ford		
	CONDUCTING	W. Waldrop	
	CALLING	Passaro	
	DECK	Athens	

Notes: 7:15p – M. Singer, wardrobe, hair – rehearse Junin costume change (need Junin Wall IN)
7:20p – E. Roger, D. Torres - Waltz

This tells the cast what to expect for the next show. It's important to make sure that everyone knows what to expect when the other actor is on. Are there any changes (lifts, props, dancing) or differences that you need to notify the cast of?

If an actor calls out of the show, the stage manager will likely notify you. If a chorus actor calls out, then a swing would go on. If a principal actor calls out, then the understudy would go on for the role and a swing would go on for the chorus track. The amount it affects you is determined by whether or not the actor has done the track before.

It helps to make a chart of your own that tells you what to address when an actor calls out. Here is an example of the men's tracks:

Pre-show rehearsals/talk-thru chart

Men

Actor	Number	Partnering/Lifts	Involved
Che	Waltz	Dance	Eva
	Money	Dance Break	A. Amber
Peron	Art of Possible	Fight	B. Little
	Charity Concert	Tango/undressing	Eva
	Dice are Rolling	Faint business	Eva
Magaldi	B.A.	Juliet lift	Eva
	B.A.	Dance break	Eva
	B.A.	Crucifix lift	Eva, A.P., N.K.
	B.A.	Playoff	Eva, A.P.
	Montage	Bed spin	M.F., M.D.B., B. L.
	Montage	Cradle lift/spin	Eva
	Montage	Crucifix lift onto bed	Eva, C.C., A.S., N.K. A.P.
George Andrews			
Eric Christian	Money	Dance break	J. Patty
Colin Cunliffe	Goodnight	Lover/make-out	Eva
	Money	Dance break	S. Morton
	Montage	Crucifix lift	Eva, A.P., A.S., N. K. Magaldi
	Montage	Attitude press	S. Morton
	Montage	Bed spin	N.K., A.P., A.S.
Bradley Dean	Art of Possible	Fight	D. Torres and B. Little
	Santa Evita	Lift	child
Const. Germanaocs	B.A.	Pencil turn lift	Eva
	Art of Possible	Fight	D. Torres
Nick Kenkel	Requiem	Mourning tango	K. Covillo
	Junin	Tango	S. Morton
	B.A.	Trio/crucifix lift	Eva, A.P., Magaldi
	Charity Concert	Tango	B. Hibah
	Money	Dance break	B. Hibah
	Money	Button lift	Eva, A.S., A.P.
	Montage	Attitude press	K. Covillo
	Montage	Crucifix lift	Eva, Magaldi, A.P., A.S., C.C.
	Montage	Bed spin/flag	A.S., C.C., A.P.
Brad Little	Art of Possible	Fights	B. Dean, Peron
	Montage	Bed spin	M. Field, M. de la Barre, Magaldi
Aleks Pevec	Requiem	Mourning Tango	B. Hibah
	B.A.	Trio/Crucifix lift	Eva, N.K., Magaldi
	B.A.	Playoff	Eva, Magaldi
	Goodnight	Lover/make-out	Eva

If he/she has done the track before, then you may have to do little, if anything, to get him/her prepared for the show. You may have to run a lift rehearsal or anything the actor has requested to the stage manager. If he/she has never done the track before, then you may have to come to the theatre earlier and work with him/her before the show.

You can go over the list with the actor and see if he/she wants to do any of it. It's also important to know if his/her partner wants to do anything, even if the actor doesn't think it's necessary. You would tell the stage manager what you want to do and when and the stage manager will contact all involved to schedule it. The schedule goes through the stage managers because there are other departments getting ready for the show at the same time. Perhaps the crew guys will have to alter their daily routine to accommodate your needs. That kind of scheduling is all done by the stage manager.

> *TIP:*
> *Be prepared to get the call at the most inconvenient time and place. You will need to act swiftly so other departments can be notified of the changes for the show.*

Cut Tracks/Combo Tracks

There will be times when you have to figure out a *cut track* or *combo track*. A *cut track* would refer to an entire track being cut from a show. A *combo track* is when another actor has to do a combination of covering two or more actors during a show. This is what you do when you have more actors out of the show than you have to cover every role. You have to decide which tracks or parts of tracks to cut for the show.

> *"I remember getting a call while I was at the grocery store. I always get a little nervous when I see stage management's number come across my phone screen. I was told that we needed to do a cut show. We had 4 chorus girls out and only 2 female swings. I was glad I had my Stage Write bible in my purse where I could start looking at the show and what cuts we would need to make."*
>
> *- Jennie Ford*

Here is an example of a dance captain making cut tracks/combo tracks:

Jess/Erica/Margot/Sydney

	Jess	Erica	Margot	Sydney
Requiem	Wendi	Jennie (DS couple then switch to Margot)	Cut (George leaves before Tango)	Cut (Daniel Leaves before Tango)
Quartet	Wendi	---	Jennie	---
Junin		---	Jennie	Wendi
BA	Cut (Laurel and constantine lead snakes)	Jennie runs on late and goes to Erica's spot	Cut	Wendi
Lovers	---	---	---	---
Art of Possible	---	---	---	---
Charity Concert	---	Jennie	Wendi	---
Another Suitcase	---	---	---	Cut hooker
Peron's Flame	Wendi	Jennie	Cut (Emily leaves before partnering)	---
New Argentina	Wendi	Jenie	Cut---	Cut
Balcony	Wendi	Jennie	Cut	Cut
High Flying	Wendi	Jennie	---	Emily (take out mirror, bring on powder puff and take mirror from Eva, give powder to Colin,
Rainbow Tour	Cut secretary (Daniel has own stuff)	Jennie	---	Wendi
Chorus	---	---	Cut	---

For the above scenario, four girls called out of the show and there were only two female swings. You start by going through each number and deciding what of each track is absolutely necessary or more important.

Take into account props, partnering, entrances and exits. Then consider how those two actors affect the rest of the company in each number. Go through each number, and make a list of what the replacement actor (swing, understudy) will do and what is cut. Then double check exits and entrances to see if it is possible. You can refer to your tracking sheets. Does the costume change work for the replacement actor.

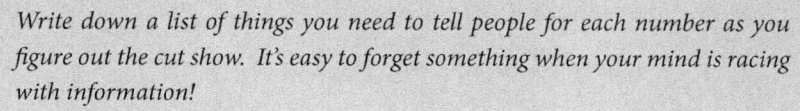

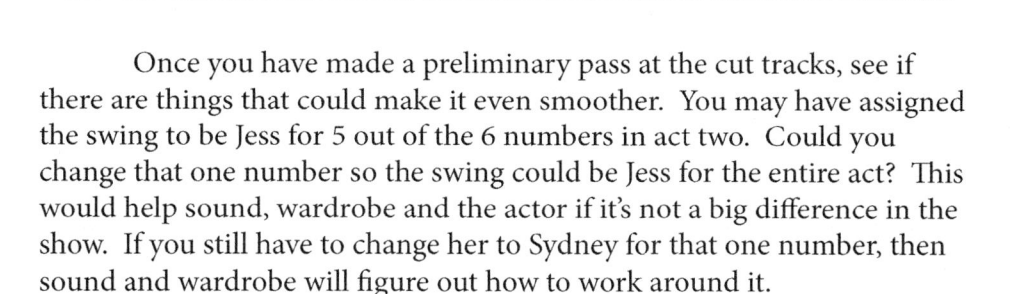

> *TIP:*
> *Write down a list of things you need to tell people for each number as you figure out the cut show. It's easy to forget something when your mind is racing with information!*

Once you have made a preliminary pass at the cut tracks, see if there are things that could make it even smoother. You may have assigned the swing to be Jess for 5 out of the 6 numbers in act two. Could you change that one number so the swing could be Jess for the entire act? This would help sound, wardrobe and the actor if it's not a big difference in the show. If you still have to change her to Sydney for that one number, then sound and wardrobe will figure out how to work around it.

When you have the final version, you can email it to stage management. It's helpful to get someone else to verify that everything you decided will work. You can ask stage management, the assistant dance captain or the swing doing the cut track, to look it over. It's a good idea to go over the cut track with the swing to make sure he/she is comfortable with the show he/she will have to perform. The swing is the one who has to perform this crazy cut show track, so be very supportive and understanding if he/she is a little more stressed than usual.

In the previous example, there were a couple instances when other actors in the chorus had to make minor adjustments, like bringing out props or leaving the stage earlier because they had no partner. Once the initial draft was done, the dance captain talked to all the actors who were affected by the changes.

You can keep the cut show track for future use if it ever happens again. Feel free to add any notes for yourself to make it better for next time. It is also good for a reference for other cut show tracks.

If cut tracks happen often, you or your deputy should contact the Equity business representative for the show. It may be in indication that your show does not have enough "coverage" and needs to hire more swings.

Now that the cut track is figured out, it will be posted on the board but the details won't be. It would be too much information to include in the notice to the full company. You need to go around the theatre to tell all those involved of the changes to expect.

> **Notes to give company for cut track June 5th**
> - Tell George and Daniel to leave before Tango in Reqium (no partners)
> - Tell Constantine he's leading everyone out in BA (no Laurel)
> - Tell Johnny to follow Christie in BA snake out (no Rachel)
> - Tell Nick, Johnny and Constantine that Sydney's hooker is cut (own business)
> - Tell Emily to leave after walk around in Peron's flame (no dance partner)
> - Tell Emily to take on mirror and powder puff (no Sydney), give puff to Colin
> - Tell Daniel to bring on own props in Rainbow Tour (his secretary is cut)
> - Tell Nick to sing from wings in Money, his dance partner is cut
> - Tell Jess and Johnny to move to center for partnering to fill space
> - Tell EVA that Emily will be giving her mirror and powder puff
> - Tell Bahiya to move to center for bows to make space even

"One night at EVITA, so many guys called out that we didn't have enough male swings to cover them all. We had to ask one of the actors to do a 'chorus adjustment' and sing one line just for that show. He was a great singer and felt confident in rehearsal singing, 'She really brightened up your out-of-town engagement'. When it came time for him to do it onstage, he had a moment of amnesia because it seemed so foreign to him. Instead, he 'sang-slurred' something like, 'She really gave you arms that ground you to the public' (if we had to guess what the words were). It made no sense and the whole company had to act like it did and try to move on without laughing. We sure laughed offstage!!!"
- Jennie Ford (Dance Captain)

On the next page, there is another extreme case where multiple actors are out. On this notice, there are notes for the sound department so they know whose mic to turn on and off during each number. It gets tricky when one actor has to cover multiple actors in one show. The sound person has to "re-patch" the microphones that are already programed into his/her console.

Here is an example where the *adjusted show notes* were posted on the callboard by stage management:

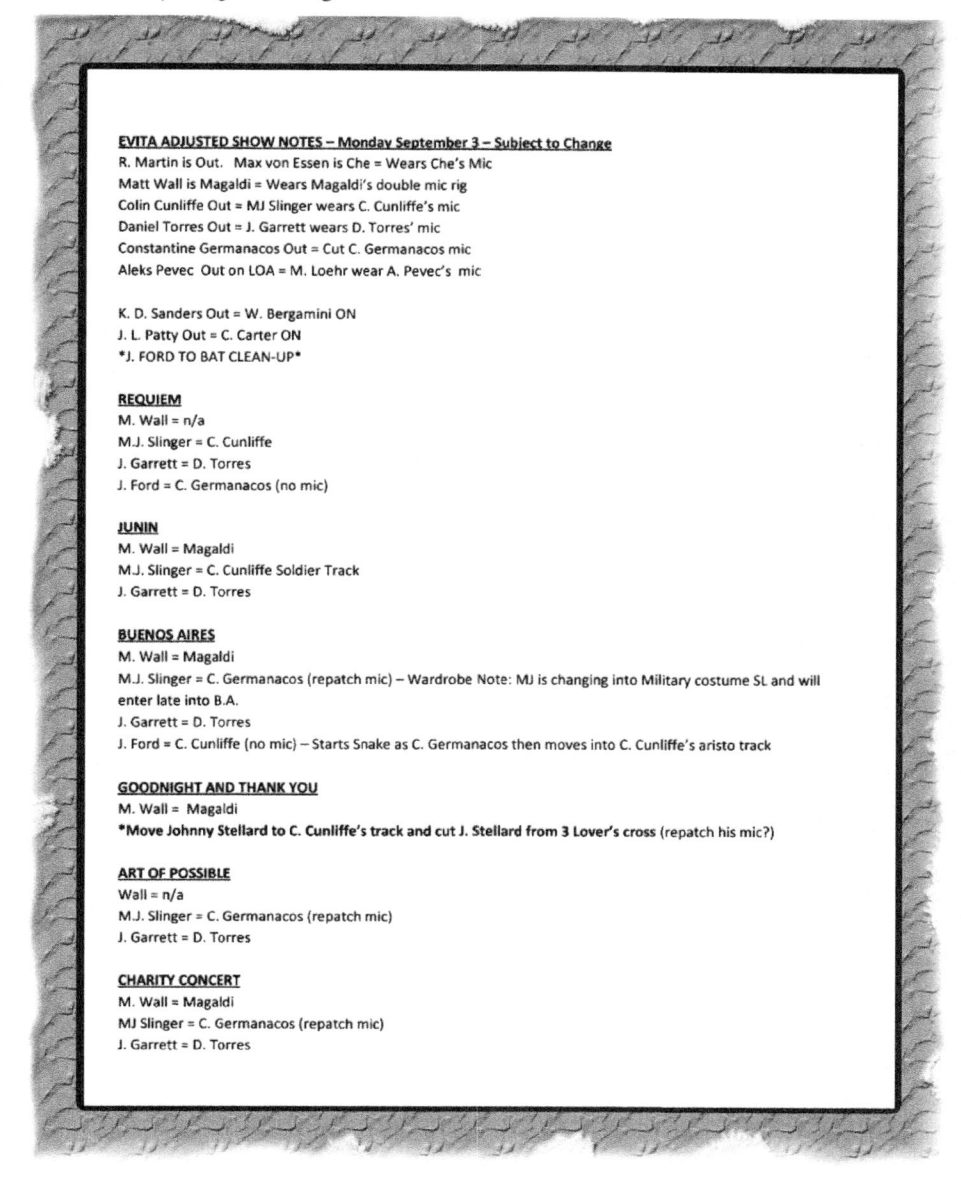

> **EVITA ADJUSTED SHOW NOTES – Monday September 3 – Subject to Change**
> R. Martin is Out.   Max von Essen is Che = Wears Che's Mic
> Matt Wall is Magaldi = Wears Magaldi's double mic rig
> Colin Cunliffe Out = MJ Slinger wears C. Cunliffe's mic
> Daniel Torres Out = J. Garrett wears D. Torres' mic
> Constantine Germanacos Out = Cut C. Germanacos mic
> Aleks Pevec Out on LOA = M. Loehr wear A. Pevec's mic
>
> K. D. Sanders Out = W. Bergamini ON
> J. L. Patty Out = C. Carter ON
> *J. FORD TO BAT CLEAN-UP*
>
> **REQUIEM**
> M. Wall = n/a
> M.J. Slinger = C. Cunliffe
> J. Garrett = D. Torres
> J. Ford = C. Germanacos (no mic)
>
> **JUNIN**
> M. Wall = Magaldi
> M.J. Slinger = C. Cunliffe Soldier Track
> J. Garrett = D. Torres
>
> **BUENOS AIRES**
> M. Wall = Magaldi
> M.J. Slinger = C. Germanacos (repatch mic) – Wardrobe Note: MJ is changing into Military costume SL and will enter late into B.A.
> J. Garrett = D. Torres
> J. Ford = C. Cunliffe (no mic) – Starts Snake as C. Germanacos then moves into C. Cunliffe's aristo track
>
> **GOODNIGHT AND THANK YOU**
> M. Wall = Magaldi
> *Move Johnny Stellard to C. Cunliffe's track and cut J. Stellard from 3 Lover's cross (repatch his mic?)
>
> **ART OF POSSIBLE**
> Wall = n/a
> M.J. Slinger = C. Germanacos (repatch mic)
> J. Garrett = D. Torres
>
> **CHARITY CONCERT**
> M. Wall = Magaldi
> MJ Slinger = C. Germanacos (repatch mic)
> J. Garrett = D. Torres

All departments are affected by the cut/combo shows. Stage management will notify wardrobe, sound, props, hair and any other department that is affected. Your job is to help the stage manager identify adjustments because you will likely have the best idea of what an actor does throughout his/her show.

A dance captain taking notes.

Illustration by Camille Bertrand

"One of these things is not like the other."

CHAPTER 14

A Day in the Life of a Dance Captain

It's almost impossible to write about "a day in the life of a dance captain". It would be difficult to capture the full scope of what we do by singling out one day. Every day is different from the next. It might be simpler to ask, "What doesn't a dance captain do?" Not only do you have to dance, but you also have to be a clear communicator, a teacher, a mediator, an organizer, a quick thinker, a problem-solver, a confidant, a multi-tasker and a good listener.

Here are some typical scenarios ranging from rehearsal to after opening:

Making a show bible: You find some stage diagrams to start notating the staging and choreography so you don't forget the details. You try to learn everyone's names quickly to notate where each actor is placed at all times. This can take weeks or months to perfect.

Tech rehearsal: The choreographer is working on a number and some actors don't remember where they go. The choreographer asks you where he placed people in the studio. You look at your bible and tell Sally she was "stage right 7 with heels on the track". The choreographer decides it could be pictured differently so every actor gets moved to a different place on the stage. You quickly notate those changes.

An actor has to go for a costume fitting during the afternoon and the swing has to step in for the first time. You work with the swing to make sure he is comfortable. You make sure he knows where to go and you help him work his partner for the first time.

Rehearsals during previews: The creative team tried a new number for 3 days and now thinks it doesn't work. The creative team wants to go back to the original number, but the actors don't remember it. You are glad you didn't throw out your old notes, because you are asked to review with the company what they did before.

"Noting" the show: The creative team has left. Now it's time to make sure their vision is maintained and every audience gets to see it as if it was opening night. You watch the show and notate what needs to be fixed. At intermission, Beth tells you Greg keeps kicking her in one number but she doesn't know why. You write it all down on your note pad for tomorrow.

Giving out notes: You arrive an hour and a half before the show because you have 25 notes to give out. You tell Steve that he could turn his head a little quicker to match the others. You tell Sally that her extra head movements look great on her, but she is now the only thing you watch onstage. Judy rushes in and although you have 5 things that she could work on, you give her one for her performance for tonight. (Then praise her tomorrow for doing it and give her the next). As you go from room to room, Lilla tells you that she doesn't feel safe in a lift. The rest of the notes wait while this becomes priority. You find her partner and rehearse the lift until both are happy. You look at your bible to see why Jim is out of the light. He is on the correct number but has migrated downstage. You tell him that if he took a big step upstage, he would be lit and all his terrific acting would not be lost. The rest of the notes will have to wait.

Don't be shy about giving out the good notes! It goes a long way. There are endless notes for improvement that go out daily but it's important for the morale of the company to remind them what they are doing right and how amazing they are!

Running auditions: You go to the studio from 10am-6pm to audition 300 actors who want to be in the show. You teach the combination and then dance with each group to help give them the best chance of remembering it. You dance full out many times to "save face" and then you go home and take an Epsom salt bath before the evening show.

Cut-shows: The stage manager calls you 2 hours before the show and says four people are out sick tonight because the flu is going around. There aren't enough actors to cover the show so you have to figure out what adjustments to make. You grab your bible and see who could be cut in each number, who manages what props and how you can get through the show. You let the stage manager know what you need to rehearse before the show to make it work. You go to the show early to tell everyone what his or her alterations will be that show.

Scheduling: To create a weekly schedule, you look at what the understudies need to learn, what the swings need help with, who is going on vacation and how to be prepared for that, and if you need to rehearse specific areas of the show that can't be fixed with notes.

Teaching replacements: You go to the theatre for 5 hours and teach Tiffany's replacement. You teach where she enters and exits the stage, where to grab props, where to change, where to stand onstage, traffic patterns, director and choreographer's intentions and other tips. There will just be you, the pianist and the replacement. You find yourself singing and dancing all the parts to help her. It makes for a lot of knowledge to be stored in your head or easily referenced in your show bible.

A dance captain's day is never dull. It's best to look at every actor as a multi-talented person who is always trying to do his/her best. It's hard to get a note when you are trying your best, so it's important to be kind and never let your ego get in the way regarding who is right or wrong.

"There have been two times that I entered a cast in an emergency as a swing. One time with Joyce Chittick as dance captain for 'The Who's Tommy' and one with someone who shall remain nameless. When I got to 'Tommy', Joyce had just been moved from the swing position into the fanciest female track. That was the only track I knew because I had done it on the road. She put me on for it for weeks while she ran around like a chicken with her head cut off doing unsexy things like striking chairs and moving other furniture. She was 21 and had the maturity and integrity to delay her debut in a wonderful track so that the show could go on safely and smoothly. When I arrived for another job in a similar emergency situation as a swing, the dance captain put herself on for her favorite tracks while I, the new person, ran around doing multi tracks, newly learned, set moves in a show I didn't know".

- Lisa Gajda *(Tuck Everlasting, Chaplin, Catch Me If You Can, Elf, Finian's Rainbow, Pal Joey, Cry-Baby, The Times They Are A-Changin', Spamalot, Taboo, Urban Cowboy, Movin' out, Sweet Smell of Success, Kiss Me, Kate, Fosse, How to Succeed in Business Without Really Trying, The Who's Tommy)*

CHAPTER 15

What Broadway People say Makes the Best Dance Captain

I decided to do a little experiment and survey the Broadway community to determine what they believed were the most important traits for being the best dance captain. I had an overwhelming response from over 60 Broadway professionals. Responses came from actors, swings, directors, choreographers, current and past dance captains.

Some words and phrases were repeatedly used to describe the best dance captain:

Organized and prepared
Approachable
Personable
Collaborative
Patient
Skilled in dealing with different personalities
Has quick, good instincts
Detail oriented
Focused on the bigger picture
Supportive and encouraging
Leader
Diplomatic

The most interesting observation from gathering the information was that rarely did someone mention being the **best dancer** or even a good dancer made someone the "best dance captain". It always came down to the personality of the dance captain and his/her ability to deal with people and situations.

Some valuable observations

"The best dance captains are what I call 'leadership chameleons'. At any time, they can be called upon to be military strategists, doting parents, math wizards, and/or behavioral psychologists; they know (instinctively or through hard-won experience) how and when to deploy these skills at a moment's notice, and with the exact calibration that properly serves whatever challenge comes their way."
- Stage manager, Michael Passaro (*Pippin, Bright Star, Wolf Hall, The River, The Testament of Mary, Evita, How to Succeed in Business Without Really Trying, Promises, Promises, A Steady Rain, Impressionism, White Christmas, Les Miserables, The History Boys, Chitty Chitty Bang Bang, A Year With Frog and Toad, Dance of the Vampires, Sweet Smell of Success, Carousel, Angels in America, The Will Rogers Follies, Aspects of Love, Phatntom of the Opera, Starlight Express*)

"Being a dance captain is like being your favorite childhood babysitter. You have to evaluate each child's personality. You need to learn what their breaking points are, when to encourage them, when to set the ground rules, and which battles to pick. The 'greatness' comes with the ability to let them have fun while keeping them in line, all the while remembering, at the end of the day you have to report to a parent."
- Dancer/singer/actor and Gypsy Robe recipient, Charlie Sutton (*An American in Paris, Kinky Boots, Lysistrata Jones, Catch Me If You Can, How to Succeed in Business Without Really Trying, Women on the Verge of a Nervous Breakdown, The Addams Family, Cry-Baby, La Cage aux Folles, Wicked*)

"The best dance captains have the ability to make the performer feel at ease while simultaneously maintaining the integrity of the show. They maintain an easy rapport with both the creative team as well as the cast. They are patient when putting in new people, and can see the big picture: what is the focus of a scene, what needs to happen with precision. They understand a swing's job is not to come in and reinvent the wheel but

to meet the other performers where they need to be met. The calmer the better. Dance captains, like stage managers, can set the tone for an entire production. The more humor, grace, and confidence they can bring to the room, the better. That is professionalism."
- Singer/Actress, Rebecca Eichenberger *(Phantom of the Opera, A Grand Night for Singing, Carousel, 1776, Ragtime, The Frogs, Evita, An American in Paris)*

"The knowledge of dance, attention to detail, great organizational skills, and a certain meticulousness are kind of pre-requisites for any good dance captain. But beyond the technical skills, and equally, if not more important, are a sense of humor and a genuine love for dancers and performers of all abilities. Knowing what someone 'needs to do' is not the same as helping, persuading or freeing them to do it. The more you can intuitively understand another performer's way of working and learning, the more you will be able to help them get past their habits, their fears, their insecurities and their defenses and allow them to live up to and grow beyond what they are capable of. If you can be an ally and an advocate as well as an instructor and 'maintainer', you'll get the best out of the people you work with--and with much less drama."
- Tony award winning actor, Michael Cerveris *(Fun Home, Evita, In the Next Room, Hedda Gabler, Cymbeline, Lovemusik, Sweeney Todd, Assassins, Titanic, The Who's Tommy)*

"The BEST dance captains are unique individuals that are respected not only for their work onstage as a performer but also their abilities to be teachers, mentors, collaborators, and in truth the BEST dance captains are often the "silent strength" of the musical. They are selfless, giving, insightful, forward-thinking people who have the ability to manage personalities in high pressure situations. The BEST dance captains are entrusted by the creative team to maintain the original vision of the musical, allowing each audience for years to come have an experience as if they were at an opening night performance."
- Associate Director/Choreographer, Tara Young *(The Little Mermaid, The Pirate Queen, Chitty Chitty Bang Bang, The Frogs, Dance of the Vampires, Thou Shalt Not, The Music Man, Contact, Ragtime, Showboat)*

"A dance captain's job is to maintain the truth and essence of the choreographer's vision. It's one of the hardest jobs to perpetuate and preserve in the theatre dynamic. Not everyone is designed for this and in my experience, not everyone has what I consider one of the most important characteristics needed. They need 'the art of their own voice' when dealing with the material or choreography and the skills in which to relay information to an original cast or, as it evolves, to new cast members. The dance captain understands the original ideas for why the choreography was created, the intention behind the moves or phrasing and the means to translate that in their own words. Not everyone learns in the same way or understands in the same way. The dance captain should be able to achieve the choreographer's vision using their own voice and be able to negotiate those moments with actors. There are many more facets to the dance captain position, but this is one of the most important and respectable qualities I look for and gravitate towards."

- Actor/singer/dancer, Timothy J. Alex *(Tuck Everlasting, Motown the Musical, Elf, How to Succeed in Business Without Really Trying, Pal Joey, Dirty Rotten Scoundrels, Never Gonna Dance, Man of La Mancha, Sweet Smell of Success, Thou Shalt Not, Chicago)*

"An awesome dance captain is someone who has an eye for detail. Someone who has a knack for teaching and breaking things down for people who don't learn as quickly. Someone who has the best interest of the show and the company at heart! Someone personable who the company feels comfortable asking questions of if they are unclear."

- Singer/actress, Sierra Boggess, (*School of Rock - The Musical, It Shoulda Been You, Master Class, The Little Mermaid, The Phantom of the Opera*)

"I am generally attracted to dance captains who are very good dancers, intelligent, organized and have the essence of a choreographer. I am always looking for people who have an understanding of detail."

- Choreographer, Sergio Trujillo *(On Your Feet!, Hands on a Hard Body, Leap of Faith, The Addams Family, Memphis, Next To Normal, Guys and Dolls, Jersey Boys, All Shook Up)*

"The qualities I always look for in a dance captain are leadership and diplomacy. They also have to be anticipatory. The dance captain always needs to change something at the last minute due to an injury or illness. They are the real unsung heros during the run of a show."

- Tony Award winning director and choreographer, Susan Stroman *(Bullets Over Broadway, Big Fish, The Scottsboro Boys, Young Frankenstein, The Frogs, Oklahoma!, Thou Shalt Not, The Producers, Contact, The Music Man, Steel Pier, Big, Show Boat, Crazy For You, Picnic)*

"The dance captains that I've admired the most have the utmost patience with actors, especially when one of them says 'that's not the way the

choreographer originally had us do it'. So patience is important, but also confidence to justify the reason behind why something needs to be rehearsed, or why something has to change. Also, the ability to listen to an actor and help find good solutions to blocking or choreography problems."
- Singer/actress, Mary Illes *(The Music Man, The Scarlet Pimpernel, Steel Pier, She Loves Me, The Phantom of the Opera)*

"The best dance captains maintain a good relationship with each actor in a show. If a dance captain has his/her 'favorites', it's important for that not to show. If a dance captain shows favoritism to some actors over others, it decreases the morale of a cast and reduces the other actors' trust of the dance captain. It would be like a parent showing favoritism to one child over another."
- Actress/singer/dancer, Tina Ou *(Wonderful Town, The Music Man, Once Upon a Mattress, Rent, The King and I, Joseph and the Amazing Technicolor Dreamcoat)*

"What makes the best dance captain for me is integrity. After opening night, the creative team leaves and the dance captain is left with a lot of power. Second to integrity is relational style. A dance captain has to know what stuff to be a stickler for and what stuff to give some room on. If a dance captain is too lenient, the cast doesn't feel well taken care of. If they are controlling, nobody respects them. Having good taste, a deep understanding of what the choreographer values, and knowing how to convey that information is of the utmost importance."
- Actress/singer/dancer, Lisa Gajda *(Tuck Everlasting, Chaplin, Catch Me If You Can, Elf, Finian's Rainbow, Pal Joey, Cry-Baby, The Times They Are A-Changin', Spamalot, Taboo, Urban Cowboy, Movin' out, Sweet Smell of Success, Kiss Me, Kate, Fosse, How to Succeed in Business Without Really Trying, The Who's Tommy)*

CHAPTER 16

Balancing the Leadership Aspect of the Position

People wonder how to manage a leadership role when working with people your age, or older. There is a basic need for a large group to have leadership of some kind. Psychologically, it is more comforting than the alternative, chaos. At the same time, not everyone wants to be a leader. A dance captain is somewhat similar to a team captain in sports. You can often find articles about what makes a good captain of a sport's team. You won't find many on being a good dance captain. However, it seems to directly translates to the "sport" or art of dancing.

The following is a list of traits that make a good team captain:

1) Organizer
2) Promotes positive thinking
3) Recognizes his/her teammates' skills
4) Ensures unselfishness for the greater good
5) Creates a harmonious working relationship
6) Takes the time to know his/her teammates personally
7) Mentors his/her teammates

This directly relates to being a dance captain on Broadway.

1) Organizer: You must be organized to be effective. It's important to find a system to record the information for the show, helping you do your job. The more organized you are, the more efficient and accurate you are. The

company will build trust in your notes and your verbal communication. If they know you keep great notes, they understand when you ask them to move to a certain "number" on the stage, it's accurate. Alternatively, if you never write anything down, they may not respect the notes you give. Someone is more likely to challenge the accuracy of your notes.

2) Promotes positive thinking: If you are in musical theatre, you know there are "demons" in everyone's head reminding him/her of his/her limitations. To get the best out of others, you need to encourage them, helping them believe they can do anything. A singer may be terrified to dance. He/she may mentally block himself /herself from learning choreography. They may silently repeat, "I can't do this! I can't dance!". Your job is to work with them, changing their mind-set, to obtain a different result. Once you help them through it, they will understand they can do it!

3) Recognizes his/her teammates' skills: It's beneficial to create the feeling that no one is better than another, including the dance captain. If you have the attitude that you are better because you are chosen as the leader, your peers will naturally want to "bring you down". If you respect everyone in the show for their own special skills, you will gain respect from your peers. It's appropriate to voice the positive traits of others and praise them in front of other peers. Comments like, "Now if only I could kick my leg up as high as Judy" or "If I could only do this while singing a high D like Hailey" can go a long way! It's positive for you, for the person receiving the compliment, and for the company who knows you respect them.

4) Ensures unselfishness for the greater good: This ability can be related to the old adage "Do you want to be right or do you want to be happy?". You may have recorded meticulous notes from the first day of rehearsal. Let's say it's as precise as "Jimmy's right foot is on 12". After a while the actor may be asked what number he is on. He may remember it as "12", even though you remember it as "right foot on 12". Now unless it's hurting anyone, do you have to stand your ground, be correct and upset with an actor over it? You don't always have to be right or perfect to be respected. It's actually the contrary. Those who can admit mistakes are looked at as stronger. It's also important to encourage unselfishness in others too. Everyone at some point wants to "stand out" but you don't want those moments to be detrimental to the show and the story. If someone is "mugging" or being "too different" then you have to find other ways for

them to feel good about what they are doing in the show.

5) Creates a harmonious working relationship: You should "be the sunshine" in the building. It's important to lead by example and always put on a pleasant face. You are the liaison for many people. You are the liaison between partnering couples, so keep the communication open and allow for an enjoyable working environment. You are the liaison between management and the company. You can empathize with the cast and speak to management on the cast's behalf if something is dangerous or tricky.

6) Takes the time to know his/her teammates personally: This is an important part of the job that can create exceptional results! When you create positive relationships, you create trust. When you express a genuine interest in people's lives, they believe you care about them. They feel "listened to" and heard. When you have something to say to him/her about the show, they will return the favor and listen to you.

7) Mentors his/her teammates: This is not as relative in a Broadway show because everyone is hired as a professional and expected to know their job. If you find that someone asks you for help, be approachable and offer any advice needed. Mentoring is by example, try to be the person you would like to work with on a daily basis.

You can also look at the cast as being part of a family. Be compassionate, a good listener, a good teacher, a mediator, and a "mom" to varied personalities. Love each person for his/her talent and capabilities. It's sometimes easier to have compassion for children than for adults. So if you have trouble with a cast mate, try looking at him/her differently. This is not to sound patronizing, only another "tool", but what if the person was a child? Would you have more empathy with him/her if you looked at them as a sensitive, impressionable child who doesn't like making mistakes? It's more about handling a situation with empathy, not about using patronizing tactics with peers. The latter always fails! Assume everyone is doing their best and continuously encourage them, so their best becomes even better. Help them believe they can do anything. Help rid actors of their fears and demons, pushing them to increase the limits of their own expectations.

The role of any captain is enhancing mutual respect and trust, while maintaining control in the most stressful situations. A good "captain" organizes and puts the success of the group ahead of personal interests. They also recognize the value and contribution of each actor, addressing situations in a positive way to come up with solutions, while preserving the company's chemistry. It's about holding yourself accountable to a high standard, giving 100% effort. In turn, you will garner the company's respect. Be a role model. You cannot cut corners and earn the respect of fellow actors. If you fulfill these duties of a captain, you will gain credibility. You don't need to be the best dancer in the show to be a good dance captain or to gain the respect of the company.

Not all these are inborn traits. They can be worked on and developed to become an extraordinary dance captain.

TIP:
A dance captain's success is related to how he or she gains the trust and respect of the cast. You are most effective when you gain the company's respect, and in return, feel appreciated for the work you do.

CHAPTER 17

Should I be a Dance Captain?

Why should I be a dance captain? It's such hard work! Yes, it is. It can be personally rewarding if you learn how to manage stress and people. There are many reasons why someone would chose to be a dance captain.

- *Learning:* The "learning part" will never cease. There will be various personalities in every company and you have to learn how to manage those differences. You will learn a lot about yourself and hopefully grow as a person as you navigate stressful situations.

- *Choreography path:* If you desire to be a choreographer, the dance captain position is a great way to learn more about what a choreographer's role is. This is most beneficial during pre-production and rehearsals before opening.

- *Recognition:* It's a symbol of recognition and trust by your choreographer to fulfill the position and represent him/her. If you do it well, you will have recognition from your peers and your stage manager. This can help you with future jobs and recommendations. It also has merit on a resume. Your name will be listed in the program on the title page so the audience knows you are the dance captain.

- *Money:* The compensation may not be a lot for the extra work you have to do. However, 20% more on a paycheck is helpful.

- ***Another career path:*** You may not have a desire to be a choreographer but you may find being a dance captain suits your capabilities. You may open up a career path as a respected dance captain on Broadway if you do it well.

- ***Challenge:*** It's a great way to challenge and exercise your mind. The memory and critical thinking requirements will challenge your brain's synapses.

> *TIP:*
> *You don't have to be the best performer to be an excellent dance captain. The position requires different skills!*

What training do I need?

You can be trained to be a dance captain, but probably the best way to practise is on the job. To help you be the best dance captain, you will need to have innate qualities that can't always be taught. If you struggle with these characteristics, then you could work on the following:

- People skills
- Patience
- Communication
- Listening
- Compassion
- Efficient problem solving
- Organizational skills
- Note-taking skills
- Teaching ability
- Leadership skills
- Understanding dance movement and music

There are dance captains hired for shows where no trained dancers are hired. Any time there is choreographed movement that goes above what the stage manager is required to learn, then an actor will be assigned as a dance captain. Although it is common practice to have dance training, formal dance training is not required to be a dance captain. In most of the big Broadway musicals, it is likely the dance captain will have dance training in the style of the choreography. You do not need a degree in dance though. A choreographer may pick someone from the dance audition or wait until the first day of rehearsal to see who to pick for the position. Most often, the choreographer will know before rehearsals start who the dance captain will be. The choreographer may wait to choose an assistance dance captain if one is needed. If you are interested in undertaking such a job, you can always mention it to the casting director during the callbacks.

Some choreographers prefer a swing be dance captain so he/she can watch the show on a regular basis. This will differ from show to show and choreographer to choreographer, but it's good to keep that in mind. For example, if you mention you want to be a dance captain for a Stroman show, you will likely be suggesting yourself as "a swing and a dance captain". Take a look at the Broadway shows currently playing to see how often the dance captain is also a swing. It's good to note who the choreographer is so you know what to expect when you audition for him/her in future.

Your Life is the Show

While you are a dance captain, you can pretty much guarantee a lot of your time will be spent at the theatre or dealing with the show. You may never have the time to get everything done you want or expect to. Just do your best.

Rehearsals

Understudy rehearsals: Once the show opens, most of the cast will have their days free with the exception of swings, understudies, stage managers and dance captains. You will be at the theatre during the day teaching the swings and understudies. Understudy rehearsal usually takes place 4-5 hours in the afternoon before a show. You will likely rehearse twice a week in the beginning, helping the understudies become comfortable with their tracks. There will be two understudies for every part and the swings will need to learn multiple tracks. It will take months to help everyone become comfortable.

Rehearsals for new cast members: There will be rehearsals with new actors that come into the show. Each actor is allowed to take a week's vacation starting 6 months after the opening night. At that time, a show may hire a *vacation swing.* This person acts as another swing and will need to be taught all the chorus tracks. This may take months. There will also be actors who leave the show and you will be required to teach their replacements. These type of rehearsals will require you to be at the theatre every day except your day off. You will likely have to teach on *the day after the day off* and be paid overtime.

Put-ins: You will also have to run put-in's for all replacement actors and that usually takes 4-5 hours on an afternoon prior to a show.

Safety rehearsals: You may be involved in a show that requires a safety rehearsal you have to run before every show. You will have to schedule "partnering rehearsals" for dancers that have new partners due to sickness or other reasons.

Phone Calls

You may receive a phone call from the stage manager, any time during the day, telling you someone is out of the show. If too many people are out, you will be required to figure out the show adjustments so the show can work. You will be responsible for helping the stage manager create "cut-tracks" if necessary.

You could be in the grocery store or eating lunch with family, but you will have to deal with the situation at hand. These moments will require you to go through the entire show, number by number, and figure out what is going to work.

The stage manager will want you to address any concerns as soon as possible so he/she can inform the cast and crew of the changes for that show.

TIP:
There will be good days and bad days. It's part of the job. Find a way to put things into perspective. Every day is a new day and you can start fresh tomorrow!

Finding a Support System

It's a challenging job and you will need to vent at times. Pick a support system that will help your reputation and not hurt it. Try not to pick people in the show or in the building to vent to. Words spoken can never be undone. You don't want your words (probably spoken in a heated moment of passion) gossiped about or misconstrued.

Take your problems elsewhere, outside the theatre. You must value your position at work and not allow gossip to jeopardize it. Give yourself time to cool down and rid yourself of some emotion that may cloud your judgment. Vent to a friend outside the show, or extended family member, or in a journal. Try not to use your partner or spouse constantly because it can wear them down. Perhaps you will need to have two or three people as your support system, so you don't keep burdening the same person with your complaints. It's wise to be professional and refrain from speaking anything confidential to anyone who shouldn't know.

Your "world" will become smaller and you have to challenge yourself to maintain perspective. You will spend so much time at the theatre with these people it will seem like nothing else is going on in the world and all the drama is at your fingertips. "It's a musical" and you have to remind yourself of that. What could be worse? A lot of things!

> *TIP:*
> *For the challenging moments when you just want to cry or scream, ask yourself, "what is my lesson here?". There is always some lesson or growing you can do in any situation that frustrates you. You can even ask the question out loud and have a laugh!*

Make sure you find time for you! This may be one of the more difficult tasks to accomplish, but it is very important not to sacrifice yourself so much that you affect the way you do your job. If you are giving too much of yourself, then your fuse will be shortened and you will become less effective. It may help to set some boundaries on your day off or on your lunch break. You may want to plan for a daily "time out". Get the stage manager on your side to also respect the moments you need away from the show and not disturb you. You may want to reciprocate the favor with the stage manager and understand what he/she needs. The stage manager's job is extremely difficult, time consuming and stressful. You want to become allies and help each other!

"As an onstage dance captain, it can be hard to solve problems that arise when your track prevents you from seeing what is actually happening onstage. There is a lot of multitasking which may involve stealing some time watching in the offstage monitor between quick changes, watching from the wings or stealing a glance while you are onstage (which can be a slippery slope). I found the need to compartmentalize so when I was onstage I was focused on my own track so I can be present for my own performance and for the safety of my partners as well, knowing full well that if an injury or something unexpected happens during the show, I can put my dance captain hat on at a moment's notice. I would build in times to my nightly track when I had breaks that I could focus on watching the show or organizing my notes. I would just keep a mental checklist as the show went on. It can really be challenging finding times and ways to give notes and have important conversations when you need to warm up and prepare for the show yourself. It's a given that you need to arrive early to the theatre. Overall, you need to rely on those around you to help you do detective work in solving problems that you can't see. This makes it even more important to have an environment of trust, openness, and honesty with the company so you can smoothly resolve issues that arise. I have learned a lot from being dance captain, it has expanded my perspective in a lot of ways." - Johnny Stellard (*EVITA, Anastasia*)

CHAPTER 18

Extras to Help you

With a little extra pre-planning, there are a few things you can do to help you with your job. These things will lessen your stress in difficult situations and help you feel like you are "on top" of everything.

Quick Rehearsal Reference

Create a chart of all the specialties (ie: safety issues, partnering) that each track requires. Then, you can quickly reference what needs to be done and with whom. You can even schedule how long you think it would take to rehearse it. (The rehearsal can differ depending on if the actor is experienced or if it's his/her first time).

The best thing is to prepare for situations such as this:
"A male dancer gets sick at the theatre and decides he can't do the show. The swing will go on for him. What are all the things you need to rehearse before the show and who does it involve? You must identify what needs rehearsal and inform the stage manager how you want to schedule it."

Swing Chart

It's your job to make sure the swings are prepared to go on for any tracks required. It's helpful to keep track of what the swings have learned, rehearsed, and performed previously.

Below is an example of a swing chart:
(who has learned, rehearsed, and performed each track)

Swing Chart as of 8/16

Female Track	Swing	Learned Track	Had Put-In	Performed
Ashley Amber	W. Bergamini	Yes	No	No
	C. Carter	No	No	No
	J. Ford	Yes	Yes	Yes
Kristine Covillo	W. Bergamini	Yes	No	No
	C. Carter	Yes	Yes	Yes
	J. Ford	Yes	Yes	Yes
M. de la Barre	W. Bergamini	Yes	Yes	Yes
	C. Carter	Yes	No	No
	J. Ford	Yes	No	No
R. Eichenberger	W. Bergamini	Yes	No	No
	C. Carter	Yes	No	No
	J. Ford	Yes	No	No
M. Field	W. Bergamini	Yes	Yes	Yes
	C. Carter	No	No	No
	J. Ford	Yes	No	No
L. Harris	W. Bergamini	Yes	Yes	Yes
	C. Carter	Yes	Yes	Yes
	J. Ford	Yes	Yes	Yes
B. Hibah	W. Bergamini	Yes	No	No
	C. Carter	Yes	Yes	Yes
	J. Ford	Yes	Yes	Yes
E. Mansfield	W. Bergamini	Yes	No	No
	C. Carter	No	No	No
	J. Ford	Yes	Yes	Yes
E. Mechler	W. Bergamini	Yes	Yes	Yes
	C. Carter	Yes	No	No
	J. Ford	Yes	No	Yes
S. Morton	W. Bergamini	Yes	Yes	Yes

Swing To-Do List

It's going to help if the swings are as prepared as they possibly can be to go on at a moment's notice. It's helpful to have each swing go through the tracks they cover and make a list of what they would need to do before going on. Then you can address those lists with the stage manager so you can schedule as much as possible before getting into an emergency situation where you have to put a swing on and they haven't done all they wanted to do yet.

Here's an example of what a swing's to-do list would look like:

Matt's to-do list	
Actor's track	
Aleks Pevec	Practice quick-change (soldier) Practice flag folding and timing (Funeral) Dancing with Erica (Money)
Alex Michael Stoll	Work with Eva and costume (soldier) Work with the trunk prop (Money) Dance with Kristine (Money and Tango) Eva's lifts (BA and Montage)
Johnny Stellard	Partner with Erica (Tango) Practice bed spin with other actors (Montage) Practice Eva's faint (Rainbow high) Eva lifts/dance (BA)
Colin Cunliffe	Sing with group (Junin) Dance with Sydney (Money)
Eric Christian	Dance with Jess (Money) Helping with Eva's quick change (Money)
Nick Kenkel	Dance with Bahiyah (Money and Tango) Eva lifts (BA)

There are some things on the swings' lists that need to be done only once, before the first time an actor goes on. There are other things that should be done every time a swing goes on, such as partnering and safety rehearsals. You want to help the swings separate their lists into what they would need to do every time and what they would only need to try once. Examples of things they may need to do only once are costume quick-changes, practicing with props, singing harmony with a group, and so on.

CHAPTER 19

Practise Exercises

You can improve certain skills that will help you be a better dance captain, preparing you for the job. This chapter will provide some ideas as to what you can expect and you can judge how well you do them.

Learning Names Quickly

Scenario: It's the first day of rehearsal and you have not met anyone in the cast. There are 20 chorus and 5 principals. The choreographer teaches one of the big production numbers on the first day. He starts to stage the number and says to the actors, "You go here. You start on that barrel. You stand upstage of this box." You have to write down everyone's position throughout the three-minute number but you just learned (or are learning) their names. There are 50 different positions throughout the number.

Practise: Work on learning names quickly. Make a memory game for yourself by cutting out pictures of a group of actors you don't know. While looking at each picture, have someone to tell you his/her name and something about each of them as you write it down. Then, using your notes, try to remember the name of the actor as you see each picture again. Or, if you're in a classroom, assign yourselves fake names and backgrounds. Create a *facebook page* of everyone's headshots. Mingle around the room and introduce yourselves. Write down anything that will help you remember them. Then, take the same *facebook page* and write everyone's name below their picture.

Here is an example of a *facebook page* made for a new Broadway show:

CAST FACEBOOK EVITA

Elena Roger — *Eva Perón*	**Ricky Martin** — *Ché*	**Michael Cerveris** — *Juan Perón*	**Max von Essen** — *Magaldi*

Christina DeCicco — *Eva Alternate*
Ashley Amber — *Female Ensemble*
George Lee Andrews — *Male Ensemble*
Wendi Bergamini — *Swing*
Callie Carter — *Vacation Swing*

Eric L. Christian — *Male Ensemble*
Kristine Covillo — *Female Ensemble*
Colin Cunliffe — *Male Ensemble*
Bradley Dean — *Male Ensemble*
Margot de La Barre — *Female Ensemble*

Rebecca Eichenberger — *Female Ensemble*
Melanie Field — *Female Ensemble*
Jennie Ford — *Swing/Dance Captain*
Jason Lee Garrett — *Vacation Swing*
Constantine Germanacos — *Male Ensemble*

Laurel Harris — *Female Ensemble*
Bahiyah Hibah — *Female Ensemble*
Nick Kenkel — *Male Ensemble*
Brad Little — *Male Ensemble*
Erica Mansfield — *Female Ensemble*

TIP:
Try to acquire a cast list ahead of time. The stage managers may make a "facebook page" which you should study the first day, as soon as you get to rehearsal. A "facebook page" has each actor's picture and name beside it. It's becoming more common that stage management makes it to help crew become familiar with the cast. If you want to get a head-start, you could make one yourself before your first day of rehearsal. There is ample information on the internet as to who will be in the cast by the time a show starts rehearsal.

- Practice Exercises -   167

If you don't have access to a *facebook page*, then a *sign-in sheet* will do. Ask the stage manager if you can have a *sign-in sheet* to write notes down to learn everyone's names quickly. Introduce yourself to each cast member and then jot down something next to his/her name that will help you remember. For example, if they are from Ohio, if they have a child, if they went to a certain college, and so on.

Below is an example of using a *sign-in sheet*:

EVITA — SIGN IN SHEET

	NAME	FRIDAY	Notes
A.A. *	A. Amber	ASHLEY	Tall Blond, Vampires, All Shook Up
	G. L. Andrews	GEORGE	Oldest. Phantom 25 yrs.
	W. Bergamini	WENDI	Other Swing
	M. Cerveris	MICHAEL	Peron
	E. L. Christian	ERIC	Hairspray. Leap.
K.C *	K. Covillo	KRISTINE	Smash. Tall. Flex Dancer.
	J. Cudia	JOHN	
	B. Dean	BRADLEY	Dk curly hair.
	C. DeCicco	CHRISTINA	Eva Alt. Talent House
M.D *	M. de la Barre	MARGOT	New Orleans. Baby girl.
R.E *	R. Eichenberger	REBECCA	
	J. A. Eyer	AUSTIN	Swing Book. Tara
M.F. *	M. Field	MELANIE	Soprano. Nurse.
	J. Ford	JENNIE	
	J. L. Garrett	JASON	Pittsburg
	C. Germanacos	CONSTANTINE	Greek.
L.H. *	L. Harris	LAUREL	Wicked Friends
B.H *	B. Hibah	BAHIYAH	
	N. Kenkel	NICK	
E.M *	E. Mansfield	ERICA	Blond. Mama Mia
EmM *	E. Mechler	EMILY	Smiles a lot.
	A. Miles	AVA	
J.P *	J. L. Patty	JESSICA	
	A. Pevec	ALEKS	Hawaii
R P *	R. Potter	RACHEL	Mistress
	E. Roger	ELENA	Eva
G. R *	G. Ruiz	GABRIELLE	Boyfriend from Canada
K.S. *	K. D. Sanders	KRISTIE	Blond. Mother of Child.
	T. Shew	TIM	
	M. Simpson-Ernst	MAVIS	
	MJ Slinger	M.J.	Australian.
	J. Stellard	JOHNNY	
	A. M. Stoll	ALEX	
	D. Torres	DANIEL	
	M. Wall	MATT	Dance Cpt. Swing
	M. von Essen	MAX	Magaldi.

Eye for detail

Scenario: You are watching the show and are responsible for giving notes to make it 'clean'. You watch the big production numbers and notate the different interpretations of the choreography. Are all the heads the same? Are all the turns happening at the same time? Are all the formations accurate?

Practise: Watch a short performance of a group's choreography (live or on TV) and write down the differences you observe. Then make a note card (on an index card) for each note you have to give. Alternatively, you could have a notebook to write all the notes in. In this case, you would create a system to know when a note was given, such as putting a line through each note or checking off a "box" at the start of a note.

Giving notes

Scenario: You have to give 35 notes to performers from the previous show. You spend an hour running around the theatre looking for the people for which the notes were intended. You run across varied personalities. Some will be easy to deal with and others will not.

Practise: You could set up a mock note session with your peers and practise giving your notes from the previous exercise. Perhaps your peers can have a little fun and challenge you to see how you handle various situations. Once it's done, the peers can give feedback on how they felt about you giving notes. They could even make suggestions as to what would work better for them, and why. You could analyze your "performance" and note ways you would improve on it next time.

Teaching

Scenario: You have to run an audition. There are "6 counts of 8" of choreography. (There is choreography to fill counting '12345678' six times) You must teach a group of kids, peers, and adults. There are some who have never danced before.

Practise: Set up a mock audition with friends and teach them a piece of choreography you have learned before. You have to command the room, be clear in your communication, be encouraging and supportive, and help them to be the best they can be (all while having fun and not getting frustrated with themselves).

Creating *Cut Tracks*

Scenario: You receive a call while you are finishing dinner with friends. It's one hour before the show. The stage manager informs you someone called in sick last minute and you have to cut one track from the show. You have 10 minutes to get back to her about which track to cut and who will cover the duties. You will also need to tell the stage manager what changes you need to rehearse before the show.

Practise: This type of exercise will be different for every track (person) that calls out of a show. If you are currently doing a production, have someone pick one person's track to eliminate and time yourself to see how long it takes you to create a *cut show*. Keep in mind all of their entrances and exits, where they change clothes, what props they use, what set pieces they move, and what partnering they do. Decide what is essential to keep and what you can cut from the show. Assign other actors to do his/her "essentials". Make a list of all the changes you need to rehearse before the show. Schedule the times for each rehearsal. Make a list of changes you need to inform other actors through notes. (These changes can be done through notes and not rehearsal).

If you are not currently in a show, look at a cast list from a previous show you have done or a show that you know very well. Have someone randomly chose one person to be out of the show. Set a timer and see how long it takes you. Then try it again with a different person out and try to beat your previous record. Then you can start to add more than one person out in a show to challenge yourself.

Figuring out what swings need with little notice

Scenario: The lead gets sick at the theatre and decides he can't do his show. The understudy will go on for the lead and the swing on for the understudy. What are all the things you need to rehearse before the show and who is involved? You must identify what needs rehearsing and inform the stage manager how you want to schedule it.

Practise: Pick a show that you have done before or a show you know well. Have someone pick one actor that calls in sick and tells you who will be going on for the show. (There may be multiple people on even if only one lead calls out. The understudy would have to go on for the lead and a swing would have to go on for the chorus part) Put together a list of all the things you will need to rehearse with the understudy and swing.

> *TIP:*
> *The best thing to do is be prepared in advance for these situations. If you already have a quick rehearsal reference (see chapter 18), you can quickly look it up in your paperwork. If not, you will have to go through the whole show and figure it out quickly.*

What would *you* do?

There are plenty of scenarios that will come up for a dance captain. There may not be a right way or a wrong way of dealing with it. Take a look at the scenarios below and write what you would do.

1) A cast member comes to you and says they are freezing cold in rehearsal and can't feel their toes anymore.

2) A cast member says they are concerned that the dance floor is not sprung (Equity mandates it for dancing) and is worried about injuries.

3) A cast member confided in you that they were going to call out to shoot a commercial. They never asked for proper permission because they felt it would be denied. They are telling you to give you a "heads up" and help you be prepared.

4) A cast member confided in you that she is pregnant. She doesn't want anyone to know yet but she wants help altering some of the dancing to be safe.

5) A cast member told you he would be leaving the show in two months. He hasn't told anyone or given his notice. He just told you privately because you are his friend.

6) You are privy to "management information" that if the show doesn't start selling better by next week, the producers will shut the show down with one week's notice.

7) You know the choreographer is not happy with a fellow cast mate, who happens to be your friend. She is being watched and noted for anything she does that could cause her to be fired.

8) One of your closest friends wants to audition for your show and asks you if he could come to the audition. You don't believe he is right for it.

9) You have been asked to mount the First National Tour of your Broadway show. It is being produced non-equity and Equity has stated that none of it's members can work for that producing entity.

10) You are an onstage dance captain and someone gets injured during the show. You have 5 minutes to change your clothes for the next scene and help assess the situation with the actor. You help the stage manager assess the actor to see if he can do the rest of the show and who will go on for him if not.

CHAPTER 20

Glossary of Theatre Terminology

10-out-of 12: There are certain rehearsal days allowed in the Production Contract called *10-out-of-12*. This means there are 10 hours of rehearsal allowed in a 12 hour span of a day without additional overtime paid. This can happen prior to the first public performance of a show.

A

AEA: (Actors' Equity Association) The association that represents professional stage actors and stage managers in live, scripted theatre. It regulates minimum salaries and working conditions.

AGMA: (The American Guild of Musical Artists). AGMA represents singers, dancers and other performers in operas and other classical music productions and concerts.

AGVA: (The American Guild of Variety Artists). AGVA represents performers in some Las Vegas showrooms, Radio City, some cabarets, comedy showcases, dance revues, circus and magic shows.

Actor minimum salary: This is the minimum salary an actor can be paid while working on an Equity contract. It is negotiated by the union and no producer can pay less. The minimum salary is different for each type of Equity contract an actor is using.

Adjusted show notes: These are notes posted on the callboard indicating what needs to change for that one particular show. This happens when there is a *cut show*. There are too many people out and actors are asked to do multiple duties they normally would not do. The notes inform the company what will happen and what is different from normal.

Alternate: An actor who is hired to regularly perform the leading role in a show, but performs less than another actor who was hired to play the leading role. The actor is often guaranteed to perform one or two, or more, performances a week.

Artistic staff: (see *Creative team*)

AS CAST: It is a term used when an actor has been hired for a job but the actual role they've been assigned may have parts yet to be determined. The creative team can decide how they want to use you in the show as they rehearse and create the show. Example: You may be asked to be the Doctor, Waiter or Mother in a scene that is not specified in your contract.

Assistant: This person helps a particular job title do its function. (Example: assistant director, assistant stage manager, assistant choreographer, assistant lighting designer)

Associate: This person is directly below, or next in line to a particular job title and helps them do his/her function. This position is higher in rank than an assistant. (Ex: associate director,aAssociate choreographer, associate lighting designer)

B

Backstage: The area behind the set, which is not seen by the audience.

Back Stage: A weekly entertainment trade publication that profiles the industry through articles, reviews and casting notices for theatre, film and television.

BC/EFA: Broadway Cares/Equity Fights AIDS is the Nation's leading industry-based, not-for-profit AIDS fund-raising and grant making organization.

Billing: This is how your name appears in advertising and publicity of the show. Your name appears in a certain font, size, and order in advertising. An actor can be *billed* above the title of the show, in alphabetical order, according to "star power" or size of the role.

Blend/Blending: This is a term used when more than one voice is singing. To have a nice blend is when all vocal parts are equal in volume and nothing in particular stands out from the rest.

Blocked/Blocking: When an actor is told where to stand, what to do and when to move. An actor is "blocked" into a scene or song. An actor's "blocking" is what he/she does during the scene or song.

Bobby pins: A hair pin made of metal used to hold the hair or the *wig prep* in place. It is a double-pronged hair clip with one side straight and the other wavy for grip. They come in a variety of colors to match hair colors.

Breakdown: This refers to the casting notice that goes out to the entertainment community, listing the specific requirements for roles in a show. It can specify what they are looking for regarding principals and chorus.

Broadway: (the street) A boulevard running through the theatre district in New York City.

Broadway: (theatre) Any show performed in one of the 40 professional theatres, with 500 or more seats, located in the Theatre District and Lincoln Center along Broadway, in the borough of Manhattan, NY.

Broadway Box: Another term for the Theatre District in Manhattan. It primarily runs from 40th to 54th street, between 6th and 8th Avenue.

B-Roll: Supplemental video footage of the show that is inter-cut with main footage or interviews for promotional purposes.

Brush-up rehearsal: A rehearsal that occurs during the run of the show. The main focus is to perfect certain choreography, vocals and staging.

Business rep: This is a business representative on staff at Actors' Equity, to be the liaison to the Broadway show and address any issues or concerns of the actors and management.

Buy-out: An employer may *buy out* an employee's contract by making a single prepayment, so as to have no ongoing obligation to employ the person. Provisions for a buy-out vary by contract.

C

Callboard: A bulletin board backstage upon which important information is placed such as: rehearsals and performance schedules, union and theater announcements, and notices intended for the entire cast.

Calling desk: This is the area where one stage manager will sit and speak (or *call*) the show cues over a headset to the rest of the crew. It will have monitors, lighting and fly rail cue switches and a place for the stage manager's calling script. It will likely be close to the stage and have direct visual access to it.

Calling script: The book full of cues the stage manager creates, to help him or her call the show over the headsets to the backstage crew.

Call time: This is the time you are personally required to be present at the theatre or studio to start working. It is listed on the rehearsal schedule and posted on the callboard the day before.

Cast: All the acting members of the company (onstage and off). The company of Actors hired for a production.

Cast recording/Cast album: The audio recording made of a production and sold commercially.

Casting director: The person(s) in charge of facilitating auditions where actors sing, dance and act for the opportunity of a job in a show. The casting director maintains files of actors who may be right for the show in the future.

Choreographer: The person who designs the dance sequences and the musical staging in a production.

Chorus: Someone who is part of the larger, supporting cast for the majority of the time in a play or musical. Also referred to as *ensemble*.

Clean track: A term used when doing a sound or voice recording. When you can record a song or measures of a song and have no interference or noises on the recording. (Papers shuffling, coughing, hearing the click track on the vocal track)

Clean-up: A rehearsal (staging, vocal or dance) in which notes are given to perfect the performance or restore it to it's original intention.

Click track: This is a synchronization tool used in musicals. Sometimes there are pre-recordings done for a musical that have to be synced during a show to the live orchestra and live singers. The musical director will put on a pair of headphones while conducting and use the pre-established metronome on the pre-recording to conduct the live show. The sound engineer will blend the sound of the pre-recorded click track and the live sound.

Combo track: When one or more actors has to be out of the show and an actor has to perform multiple roles/tracks because of it. Oftentimes, the swings will perform a 'combo track' when they have to take on the duties of more than one person in the same show.

Company manager: Someone who works for the general manager in charge of many daily aspects of the company. This includes (but is not limited to) dealing with performer's contracts, coordinating travel and housing, paychecks, arranging company show ticket reservations, and acting as the liaison between Equity and the company.

Comps: Tickets provided to an individual with no charge.

Cover/Covering: Term used in reference to being responsible for knowing another person's track. You may be told "You will cover Henry" or "You cover the female dancers".

Chart: A piece of paper with the stage diagram on it and other useful information about the production.

Creatives (Creative team): This is a term that lumps together the decision-makers of the show. It could include the director, choreographer, designers and any of their associates or assistants.

Cut show: A slang term meaning someone is not performing in that particular show and one or more tracks/roles in the show will have to be removed. The show will be performed without the full amount of actors onstage as it was intended.

Cut track: When an actor has to be out of the show and his/her role is removed from the show. If that actor had lines or other contributions to the show's plot, then other actors will perform those special duties instead. Oftentimes, the swing will perform a *cut track* which means he/she will have to perform the role of more than one person during the show, depending on what is most important for the show. (Also sometimes referred to as a *combo track*)

D

Dance belt: This is an anatomically supportive undergarment worn by males while performing. It hugs the genitalia snugly in place against the lower abdominal area to prevent pain or injury while performing. Most dance belts are of thong design but there are some manufacturers that have full bottom versions.

Dance captain: This is the actor/dancer selected to rehearse all replacements and understudies. He or she is responsible for ensuring that the dances run smoothly throughout the run of a production.

Dance supervisor: A person hired to maintain the choreography of one or more productions of a show. This person would be in charge of the resident choreographer and the dance captains, once the choreographer leaves the show after opening night.

Dark day: The day off or the day of rest during the workweek.

Dark house: This refers to a theatre not currently in use.

Dark night: This refers to the night of the week in which there is no performance.

Day-after-the-day-off: Every actor is entitled to one day off during the workweek. The day after the day off has restrictions as to when and what you can rehearse before you return back to work.

Day off: This refers to one day of rest during the work week where an actor will not be rehearsing or performing. (also referred to as the *dark day*).

(The) Deck: Another term for the floor of the stage.

Deluge curtain: This is a fire curtain or safety curtain for precaution used in large proscenium theatres. It is usually made of iron or heavy fiberglass and is located right behind the proscenium arch. In some older theatres it is water that is stored and poured down in heavy amounts. The purpose is to protect the audience if there was ever a fire to start onstage.

Deputy: The cast of each production must elect a deputy or deputies to serve as a liaison between Equity and the company, to ensure the upholding of union regulations.

Director: The person who gives the actors blocking during the rehearsal process, and who works with them on such things as interpretation.

Double overtime: A payment of two times the applicable contractual overtime rate as set forth in the Equity agreement. There are times when an actor gets paid *double overtime* depending on when he/she is asked to rehearse.

Downstage: A direction term that is used. The direction of *downstage* is towards the audience when you are standing onstage. The term originated when stages were raked or sloped towards the audience and you literally had to walk down the stage.

Dresser: This person assists the actor in putting on and removing costumes pieces. Broadway has union dressers, and actors do not do up each other's zippers to be helpful. The costumes cost many thousands of dollars and dressers are more experienced with garments if something were to get caught or torn. Actors, who try to help, may inadvertently harm something, and therefore, should not interfere with the dresser's job.

Dress rehearsal: Usually the last rehearsal before the play is to be performed before an audience. This rehearsal is usually done with full costume and technical effects being used, and the play is performed straight through without stopping.
Dressing rooms: The place backstage where the actors apply make up and put on costumes. Usually there are many dressing rooms to accommodate different leading roles, secondary roles, female chorus, male chorus and juvenile actors.

Dues: The fee paid by members to enable their union to represent them in negotiations, grievances, work site issues and legislative priorities. Basic dues are paid twice a year. Working dues are a percentage of your salary and are paid on a weekly basis.

E

Ensemble: This is another term meaning *chorus*. It's a group of complementary actors who contribute to a single effect of supporting the story of the play or musical.

Equity Business Rep: The staff member of the union, Actors' Equity Association, who is assigned to be the liaison between a show and the union. Each show as a *business rep*.

Equity contract: The term refers to a union contract that an actor has while performing in a show. When an actor is "on an Equity contract", he/she (along with the producer) must abide by the rules and regulations negotiated by the performer's union, Actor's Equity Association.

Equity Required Calls: The union, Actors' Equity Association, requires certain auditions to happen to help it's members gain audition access for job opportunities. Equity puts requirements such as making sure a show has chorus auditions every 6 months, whether they need to hire more actors or not.

Extension: It is a dance term denoting movement of limb away from body. If someone has "good extension", it usually means they are flexible. It can also be used as a contractual term. In this case, it would mean moving the contract end date so it would be longer than originally intended.

Extra: A person hired to provide atmosphere and background only. An Extra may not be identified as a definite character, either singly or within a group and may not be required to change make-up. An Extra may, however, make a single costume change. An Extra may not be rehearsed more than two weeks before the first public performance, may not speak except in omnes, may not sing (except with the consent of Equity in relation to a particular play), dance, or understudy and may not tour except with a pre-Broadway tryout of eight weeks or less.

Extraordinary risk: This is a contract rider that indicates you are doing something "riskier than normal" on stage. It puts a flag up for the Workman's comp insurance company, to allow for supplemental Workman's comp payments if an actor was to get injured while performing something that was deemed extraordinary risk.

F

Facebook page: This is a slang term that has nothing to do with "Facebook" as we now know it. A *Facebook page* is a page of pictures (or headshots) and the name of each actor in a show. It's usually made by the stage manager and given to the crew so they get to know who the actors are at the beginning of a new production.

Favored Nation: The wages and/or terms of one actor's contract cannot be less than that of other cast members. This is a contract rider.

Fight call: This is a rehearsal where the actors practise choreographed stunts or fights of a show. (also referred to as *Safety Call*)

Fight captain: This is the actor designated to rehearse all fight sequences with the current cast, replacements, and understudies. This person, with the assistance of the stage manager, insures that the fight sequences are properly maintained throughout the run of the production.

Fly rail: The system of steel rails, ropes and counterweights in a theatre. It is mounted close to the walls and ceiling. Everything from curtains, sets, and lights are hung on these rails. Sometimes the rails are also used for aerial stunts done by performers. The rails are lowered and raised throughout the show by automation or a crew person and a series of counter-weights.

Fourth wall: A term used in theatre to represent the imaginary wall at the front of the stage separating the audience from the performers. To "break the fourth wall" means to address or speak directly to the audience.

Frozen: A term used in reference to the show. If a show is *frozen*, there will be no more changes made to the show. This is usually done close to opening or before the critics come to see the show.

Full out/Full voice: A term used when performing or rehearsing choreography and songs. It is assumed you will perform any lifts and extensions at their fullest and you are dancing the moves as if you were performing for an audience. It also means you will sing as if you were performing for an audience.

G

General manager: Works for the producer and runs the business of the production, such as: issuing checks, keeping records, booking rehearsal facilities, and dealing with all departments.

Ghost light: This is the one light plugged in and left onstage when all other lights in the theatre have been shut off. There are many conflicting thoughts as to whether this originated out of superstition or function.

GMA: An acronym for the Good Morning America television show on the ABC network. Many shows perform on this show because of the viewership and it shoots right in Times Square.

Green room: A room backstage where the actors can lounge or await their entrance cues to go onstage. It can be one of the few areas people can eat in as well, although not every theatre has one. Eating backstage in other areas of old theatres can encourage the migration of mice, cockroaches and rats.

Guest list: This is a list that is kept at the stage door for every performance, informing the doorman who to expect and who to let in the theatre. If you have a guest who wants to see you backstage after the show, you should write your guest's name on that list.

Gypsy: This is a term that refers to a chorus actor. The term *gypsy* came from the idea that chorus actors would perform in many different Broadway shows and go from show to show.

Gypsy Robe: A long-standing Equity chorus tradition. The chorus person with the most Broadway chorus contracts will be presented with the Gypsy Robe on opening night. More information may be found on the Actors' Equity website (http://www.actorsequity.org/AboutEquity/GypsyRobe/gypsyhistory.asp)

H

Half-hour: At half-hour before curtain time, all actors in the production are to be in the theatre. It is extremely important that all actors be backstage by this time to make sure everyone is accounted for and the production can start on time. There will be a *half-hour call* made by stage management over the backstage speakers and they will check the callboard to make sure every actor has signed in by that time.

House: A term that refers to the seats in the theater where the audience sits. You will hear phrases like "Come and sit in the house" or "No food or drink in the house".

House board: A board upon which the names of the cast may be displayed. This board is either located in the front of the theatre or in the lobby.

House left: A directional term used. The direction of house left is "to your left" when you are in the audience and looking to the stage.

House lights: The lights that illuminate the audience section of the theatre to aid them in getting to and from their seats. These lights go off during a show.

House manager: The person who oversees the box office and ensures the seating and exiting of the audience. The theatre itself employs this person.

House right: A directional term used. The direction of house right is "to your right" when you are in the audience and looking to the stage.

House seats: These are considered the premium tickets or the best seats in the house. The theatre holds them for special purposes, and they won't be released to the public unless they know the seats won't be used. The cast may request and purchase these seats through the company manager. There are a finite number of these seats per show and the cost and availability differs with each production.

I

IATSE: (International Alliance of Theatrical Stage Employees). This is the union that represents the backstage crew.

Increment: A certain dollar amount that will be given to you above your contractual salary for additional duties assigned to you.

Initiation fee: The initial amount it costs to join a union and become a member.

In/out sheet: This is a piece of paper posted on the callboard before every show indicating who is *out* of the show, and who is *in*, or replacing that person.

Intermission: The time between acts when the audience can get up to use the restroom, and the actors can rest or change into their next costume. Sometimes there are scenery changes that happen during this break in preparation for the next act.

J

Just cause: Termination for a valid reason. The producer has the obligation to give the actor written notes of his/her failures and must give the actor the opportunity to correct them. If there is a dispute, the termination is subject to grievance (where applicable) and/or arbitration.

L

Lav (Lavalier): This is a hands-free amplification system consisting of a small microphone and a transmitter that an actor will wear during a show. The mic can be concealed in the hair, below the wig, attached to glasses, hats or a piece of clothing. The transmitter would be worn either in the wig, or on the actor's body in a mic belt.

League of American Theatres and Producers (a.k.a. The League): A trade association that is made up of the producers on Broadway that collectively bargain the Production Contract with the performing unions.

Load in & Load out: The first term refers to placing the set and equipment in the theatre and on the stage for a performance. The latter refers to removing the set and equipment from the theatre.

M

Management: This refers to a group of people who are in charge of running the show. It usually refers to the financial decision makers, such as producers and general managers of a show. Sometimes, people may also include other decision makers, such as stage managers, dance captains and the creative team when using this term.

Mark/Marking: A term used when you physically/vocally move through the choreography/song but you don't perform the routine to its maximum amount. It is assumed you will not attempt the lifts or do anything that may put too much strain on your muscles or ligaments. This is used when the dancers' muscles have "cooled down" or when it is only necessary for blocking purposes to see where you need to be. It may be used as a "safety run" to give you some practise before trying it full out. When working with a partner, it's important to discuss what this term means to each other so one person doesn't attempt something and catch the other off-guard. It is also used for singers when the vocal chords are not warmed up or when the song is demanding on the voice and doing it repeatedly, at *full voice*, may harm vocal chords. This term is also used for a specific place to be on the stage. For example, the director might say "Hit your marks" or "Be on your mark". This means that you have been given a specific place to be on the stage and that is your *mark*.

Matinee: A performance given during the day.

Mic belt: This is a pouch (attached to an elastic belt) that the actor wears to conceal the transmitter for a microphone. It can be worn on the waist, thigh, ribs, between the breasts, or anywhere that is comfortable.

Mic tape: This is a special, clear adhesive tape used to attach the microphone chord to the actor's skin to prevent it from bulging out. It is commonly used on the back of the neck.

Mic-up: A term used when the cast is asked to put microphones on for a rehearsal/show. The cast makes their way to the mic table, dressing room or other location to put on their mics. If you are not in costume, you may need to get a mic belt from wardrobe in order to hold the mic pack while rehearsing. There are also different options for attaching the mic in your hair, hat, or glasses. The sound department will discuss different ways with you to find the best option. There may be an elastic that goes around your head, or a hair/toupee clip that clips into your hair, or a bobby pin.

Musical director: The person who teaches the actors their songs and sets the tempo of the delivery of songs. He/she usually conducts the orchestra and the actors during every performance.

Musical supervisor: This person is hired to maintain the music (orchestral and vocals) of one or more productions of a show. The musical director and/or conductor would report to him/her.

N

National Tour: The title given to a touring production of a Broadway show.

Non-performing actor: Someone who is not in the show every night, such as a swing, standby or a dance captain.

Notice: This is a piece of paper that management can put up on the callboard to announce the closing date of a production.

Number: This can be a measurement on the stage, such as stage left 5 or stage right 18. It can also be used to describe a scene from a musical, such as "Exit stage left when you finish the number". Number usually refers to a song and/or dance scene and not a book scene.

O

Off Broadway: Productions done in Manhattan, but away from the central theatre district, and refers to theatres with seating capacities of 499 or less. The categories of Off-Broadway theatres are determined by seating capacity.

Omnes: The whole cast; everyone; all.

Open call: An audition held for a show in which anyone can attend. If the open call is an Equity call, then Equity performers are given preferential treatment and have regulations as to how the audition is run. If there is time and all of the Equity performers have been seen, the non-Equity performers may be seen.

Opening: (Often referred to as *opening night*) This is a particular performance the producers choose to announce their show officially to the public. It's considered the final and best version of the show, after weeks of changes in previews. The work of creating the show is considered over and now the show will just be performed regularly, as it is on opening night. This used to be the night when all the press came to review the show. Now, the press often comes in the few days prior to *opening* and releases the reviews after the official *opening* performance.

Out: An actor is considered *out* of the show if he/she cannot perform the show that night due to illness, vacation or other reasons preventing them from performing.

Out-of-town-tryouts: (see *Tryout*)

Overtime: Work that extends beyond the contractually allowable hours and usually involves some additional payment.

P

Part: (Part vs Role) A part is a piece of a role. These two terms can mean different things depending on the contract.

Parts determination: This is a list made when a representative of Actors' Equity comes to see the show and determines what "parts" of each actor's roles require certain recognition and payment, as well as determining "set move" payments, and extraordinary risk.

Per diem: In addition to salary, the producer pays each actor a set amount for living expenses for each day the actor is away from home or on tour.

Performing actor: Someone who is in the show every night.

Personal leave: Excused days off for reasons important to the individual worker, such as getting married.

Pin curls: This is a hairdressing technique used under wigs to secure the wigs to your own hair. If the hair was left straight, there is a chance the wigs could slip off. This is a technique to curl the hair and then fasten it to the scalp using bobby pins. This creates knobs or areas for pins to fasten the wig to the head.

Pink contract: This refers to the color of the paper of the contract a chorus member signs. It's synonymous with a chorus contract.

(The) Pit: The area (often times below the stage) where the musicians sit and play during a show. There is a special area or podium where the conductor stands, in order to be seen by all the musicians and all of the actors onstage at the same time.

Place of engagement: The city in which the show is performing.

Places: This is a term you will hear the stage manager call over the PA system and in the wings, when it is time to start the show. All actors are called to the stage area to take their positions for the top of the show.

Playbill or program: The program the audience receives which contains the actors bios, pictures, as well as the names of the production team.

Players Guide: A directory of actors utilized by casting directors, producers, etc. It includes the actors' picture, credits, union affiliation and representation.

Point of organization: The city designated as the home base for a tour. It is limited to either New York, Chicago, Los Angeles or San Francisco. If you are performing outside of the "point of organization", then you are entitled to per diem.

Press agent: The person hired by management to advertise a production through setting up interview sessions, photo shoots, etc. This person or agency is hired to create excitement and interest in seeing the show for audiences so they buy tickets.

Pre-production: The period of time during which work is done on a show prior to the first rehearsal.

Pre-set: This is the time when the crew gets the technical elements (scenery, props, lighting, sound) ready for a show. It happens before each show and the length of the pre-set is different for each show, depending on how many technical elements are used. The crew may do things, such as set flags in starting position, put props in their starting position, move scenery across the stage to it's starting position, and so on.

Preview: Performances done for an audience prior to the official opening of the show, or before critics review a show. Changes in the play may occur during this period.

Principal: A category of employment in an Equity contract. The other two are chorus and stage manager.

Producer(s): This is a person or group of people who put together a production team and the financial backers; they generally oversee the business associated with mounting a show.

Production Contract: The contract for actors administered by Actors' Equity Association used for most Broadway shows and some National tours.

Production supervisor: This is a person hired to maintain the direction of one or more productions of a show. The stage manager and resident directors would report to him/her.

Prompt book: The stage manager's book in which the blocking and technical cues are written. It is also referred to as a calling script.

Props: There are three distinct types of props; (a) hand held props actors either bring on stage with them or handle while on stage; (b) set or scenic props that are large and placed on stage before the beginning of the play or scene by the crew: (c) dress props are items placed on stage to give the illusion of reality.

Proscenium: This is the area of the theatre surrounding the opening of the stage, located in front of the scenery. This creates a "window" for the audience so the performers don't have to move around the stage to give a good view from all sides.

Put-in: A rehearsal conducted for a show already in production, to incorporate a new cast member, swing or understudy. The new actor goes through the entire role, sometimes in costume, with all the cast members (not in costume) and all of the technical elements that affect the new actor's track.

Q

Quick-change: This is when an actor has a short amount of time to change costumes, wigs, and/or shoes. Usually the actor is assisted by a dresser to help facilitate the change. The time can range from a few seconds to about 30 seconds for a full costume, wig and shoe change.

Quick rigged: This is when articles of clothing or shoes are altered to help facilitate a quick change. Shoes that used to have buckles may be changed to a hook or elastic. Shirts that look like they have buttons may have velcro hidden instead. Skirts and pants may have snaps or velcro instead of buttons and hooks.

R

Raked stage: A stage that is slanted downwards toward the audience.

Retroactive pay: Wages due for past services, frequently required when wage increases are made effective as of an earlier date, or when contract negotiations are extended beyond the expiration date of the previous agreement, or when parts determinations are made.

Rider: Special contract provisions are called riders. They generally immediately follow the face of the contract.

Role: (Role vs Part) A sum of all the *parts* an actor plays. These terms can mean different things, depending on the contract.

Resident director/choreographer: A person who is contracted to maintain the show after the director and choreographer leave. They would usually take care of teaching direction and/or choreography instead of the stage managers and/or dance captains. Not every show hires this position.

Ross Reports: This is an entertainment resource book that is published monthly in New York and it contains a detailed listing of talent agents, casting directors, commercial producers and advertising agencies. This publication is primarily geared toward film and television.

Rule book: Each of the contracts that Actors' Equity Association administers has a rule book, which lists all of the terms and conditions allowable under a specific contract.

Run-of-the-play: The dates that a show is open, which is dictated by ticket sales. The closing of the show is not a date known or specified; it is something that will be determined as the show sells.

Run-through: This is a rehearsal where the actors combine a number of scenes and/or songs together without stopping. A run-through is often referred to practising performing the whole musical or play. However, you can also have a *"run-through* of act 1" or a *run-through* of multiple sequences in a show. The goal is to not stop.

S

SAG-AFTRA (Screen Actors Guild -American Federation of Television and Radio Artists): The union that represents actors, dancers, announcers, DJ's, puppeteers, program hosts, news writers, news directors, stunt performers, broadcast journalists, recording artists, voice-over artists, and other media professionals in radio, TV, Film, internet and other media.

Safety call: (also see *Fight call*) A rehearsal when stunts are fights are practised.

Scale: Minimum salary for services under a union contract. This amount is dictated by the union and can change from contract to contract and year to year.

Scene: A unit of dialogue in a play or musical that portrays a certain situation. Plays and musicals are made up of many scenes.

SDC (Stage Directors and Choreographers Society): This is the union that represents Broadway directors and choreographers.

Secret vote/secret ballot: When you individually write your decision down on a piece of paper and it is counted anonymously. This is usually done at a meeting called by the Equity deputy where the assembled cast votes on a production related matter.

Set designer: The person responsible for designing and overseeing the construction of a stage set.

Sexual harassment: Any unwarranted or repeated sexual comments, looks, suggestions or physical contact that creates an uncomfortable working environment.

Show bible: A term used for the collection of information pertaining to that show. Also referred to as *the bible*.

Show curtain: The large curtain, usually heavy fabric, that rises at the beginning of a show to let the audience know the play or musical has started. The show curtain will rise at the beginning of each act and lower to the stage at the end of each act.

Sign-in (sheet): By *half hour*, all the actors must sign in on a sheet posted on the callboard. All the actors' names will be typed out, and the actor has to initial beside his/her name when they enter the building. Once you sign in, you must remain in the building so that stage management can reach you over the PA system.

Sitzprobe: A seated rehearsal where singers sing with the orchestra, focusing integration of the two groups. It is often the first rehearsal where the orchestra and singers rehearse together. The musical director will run the rehearsal and no blocking or movement is done.

Space-through: This is a rehearsal where the actors are "talked through" their blocking. by someone in charge (director, choreographer, stage manager, dance captain). In a musical, the actors talk through their blocking before running it with the music in case they have to stop for clarification or ask questions. (also referred to as a *Walk-through*)

Specialty: This is when a chorus person is asked to do a featured dance, vocal or acting bit within a play/musical that makes them stand out from the rest of the chorus. It's usually something that propels the story forward and is recognizable to the audience.

Split-track: When someone has to perform more than one track during a show. This occurs when more than one actor is out and the most important parts of each of their tracks get combined and performed by one person.

Spot lights: These are the bright lights that are usually controlled by technicians during the show. The purpose is to have a brighter light on someone or something, to draw the audience's attention.

Stage door: This is the actors' and employees' entrance to the theatre. A person or video camera guards it. This is where you enter and exit the theatre daily.

Stage doorman: The person who guards the stage door and who knows the reason everyone comes in and out of the theatre. He/she is there for security reasons.

Stage left: A directional term that is used. The direction of stage left is "to your left" when you are onstage and looking out into the audience.

Stage manager(s): Someone who maintains the prompt book/calling script and is hired to call the show. There will be one head stage manager and many assistants to help. They will organize the daily schedules, help run rehearsals, teach staging, manage props personnel, and oversee set moves and scenery. They also uphold the union rules and rights by keeping track of rehearsal hours, break times, etc.

Stage right: A directional term that is used. The direction of stage right is "to your right" when you are onstage and looking out into the audience.

Stand-by: Someone who learns the track of a principal role but is not part of the performing cast. This person is usually hired specifically to cover a principal role that is one of the main leads. Some productions will ask the stand by to stay backstage during a show and others will have him/her be within close proximity to the theatre and be reachable in a moment's notice.

Step outs: This is an older term not often used anymore. It means the same as a *specialty*. It's when a member of the chorus has a vocal, dance or acting feature.

Straight overtime: *Straight overtime* is just the regular overtime rate as set forth in the Equity agreement when an actor is due payment for working more than the allotted hours in the rule book. (also see *Double Overtime*)

Supplemental Worker's Compensation: Coverage that supplements workers' compensation/disability benefits. The state administers a certain amount of funds when an actor is injured on the job. This supplemental insurance is paid directly by Actors' Equity Association and can help pay more to bridge the gap between what the state pays and what the actor would be paid if he/she were still in the show receiving their full salary.

Swing (full): A non-performing member of the chorus who learns the tracks of the performing members of the chorus and performs them when said chorus is not able to perform his/her own track.

Swing (partial): A person in the performing chorus who learns the tracks of the other performing chorus members for specific *numbers* or scenes. For example: if someone got hurt during the scene before, the partial swing would already be in wig and costume and be able to step into any chorus track for the next number.

Swing (vacation): A Person who is hired when an actor is out of the show for any number of reasons (vacation, injury, personal days). This person is hired on an "as-needed" basis. They are not full time and may be asked to work in different companies of the same show, such as Broadway, National Tours or International productions.

Swing (universal): A person who is hired by a producer when there are multiple companies of the same show. They are hired full time and would go from company to company if the shows were on tour and/or on Broadway. They can be asked to go wherever needed, which could take them out of New York City, the State, or the Country.

Swing out: When a swing is put onstage for a show to cover a chorus track while that chorus person sits in the house to watch the show. Some shows do *swing outs* for each cast person to get a chance to see the show. Some shows do regular swing outs to help the chorus' bodies get a little rest and hopefully help with the physical health of the company. Some shows do not do swing outs because the creative team prefers to have the original cast onstage and minimize variables unless absolutely necessary.

T

Table read: When the company sits around a table to read (and possibly sing) through the entire play or musical. The purpose is for everyone in the room to hear the entire show in order to understand it better, without having to stand up and perform it on a stage or in a rehearsal room. This is often done in the beginning of a rehearsal process.

Tannoy: This is a term used for the public-address system in a theatre in which you can hear the stage manager's calls and announcements. Each dressing room usually has its own speaker with a volume control.

Tech (rehearsal): The is when a show practises the technical elements before an audience comes. It can typically last anywhere from 5-10 days. The director will slowly work through the show from "top to bottom" introducing scenery, lights and other technical elements for the first time. Once the technical elements get introduced, the director will start to run the show so the crew and cast gets used to the show's technical elements before getting in front of an audience.

Term contract: This is a contract with specified employment lengths. It can be a term where the producer asks the performer to stay for a certain amount of time within the run-of-the-play in exchange for extra payment. It could be a term where the producer and actor have a contract until a certain date, at which time it may or may not be renewed.

Time-and-a-half: An *overtime* payment of one and a half times the applicable contractual overtime rate as set forth in the Equity agreement. There are times when an actor gets paid *time and a half* depending on when he/she is asked to rehearse. (also see *Straight Overtime* and *Double Overtime*)

Title page: The page of a *PLAYBILL* that lists information about the production.

TKTS: This is a ticket booth in Times Square operated by the Theatre Development Fund which sells discounted theatre tickets on the day of the show.

TONYS: The awards granted by the American Theatre Wing and the Broadway League. The proper name is the Antoinette Perry Awards, for outstanding excellence in theatre. It is named after Antoinette Perry, a legend in American theatre and cofounder of the American Theater Wing. The first award was given in 1947.

Toupet clips (wig clips): These are clips that are used to fasten the mic chords to an actor's hair. They come in multiple colors to match the color of the hair/wig.

Track: Refers to the collective performance aspects of one chorus person. A swing may be required to learn multiple tracks.

Trail: This is a term used when one actor wants to follow another actor backstage throughout the course of a show. It's referred to as "trailing an actor". It is used when understudies or swings want to see the entrances, exits, prop, sound, wig and costume change details of an actor they are responsible for covering.

Tryout: This term is often used for *out-of-town tryouts*, when a Broadway show goes out of town to mount the show first. This allows for changes to be made away from the Broadway critics before coming to Broadway with a show.

Turnaround: The number of hours between the end of work on one day and the beginning of work on the next day.

Tutor: The person hired to teach school-aged children. This person is often used during the rehearsal period when the children have to be accessible by the production and yet put in a certain number of school hours.

U

Underdress: This is when an actor puts on multiple layers of costumes to assist in a quicker costume change. An entire new costume or part of a costume can be worn under the current one onstage.

Understudy: A member of the chorus who learns the track of a principal role and who is prepared to perform the role, should the actor portraying the role be unable to perform.

Unemployment insurance: Monetary contributions are made by the employer on the employee's behalf to the state fund. Should the employee be dismissed or the show close, they may receive unemployment benefits for a specific period of time.

Upstage: A directional term that is used. The direction of *upstage* is away from the audience when you are standing onstage. The term originated when stages were raked or sloped towards the audience and you literally had to walk up the stage.

V

Valuables: There may be a *valuables* collection done before the show by stage management. Any actor can turn in wallets, rings, watches, or anything of value (within limits) to be locked away in a safe place during the show to avoid theft.

W

Walk-through: This is a rehearsal where the actors are "talked through" their blocking. by someone in charge (director, choreographer, stage manager, dance captain). In a musical, the actors talk through their blocking before running it with the music in case they have to stop for clarification or ask questions. (also referred to as a *Space-through*)

White contract: Term used to refer to the color of the paper signed by an actor doing principal work.

Wig cap: This is a nylon cap that is placed over a "prepped head" (pin curled or wrapped). It secures the wig prep in place and helps secure the pins used to attach the wig to the actor's head.

Wig glue: An adhesive used to attach the lace of a wig onto the actor's skin. This helps hold the wig lace in place and prevents the lace from sticking out. It is removed by rubbing a cotton ball soaked in adhesive remover over the glued area. Wig glue is always put on by hair department personnel and not the individual actor.

Wig prep: A technique used to prepare the actor's hair for securing a wig. It can be done with pin curls and/or a combination of wrapping the hair.

Work rules: Rules regulating on-the-job standards and conditions of work in the collective bargaining agreement. Work rules are negotiated between the union and management.

Work week: The Equity work week runs from Monday to Sunday, with Thursday being the pay day.

Workers' compensation insurance: Insurance supplied by the producer to cover medical expenses that result from an on-the-job injury.

Wrangler: The person hired by the producer to be the guardian of the juvenile actors during the performance. Parents of juvenile actors are not allowed to be backstage after half hour or during a show.

Index

A

ACCA (Advisory committee on chorus affairs) 6
Alternate 20
Asking for help 22
Assistant choreographer 13
Assistant dance captain 5
Assistant musical director 13
Assistant stage manager 13
Associate choreographer 13
Associate director 13
Associate musical director 13
Auditions 129

B

Backstage business 34
Bible. *See* Show bible
Broadway musical heirarchy 13
Brush-up rehearsals 114

C

Charts 57
Choreographer 13
  assistant choreographer 13
  associate choreographer 13
  dance captain and choreographers 37
    handling conflict 41
    when to contact 42
  resident choreographer 13, 19
Choreography 5, 75
Combo tracks 135
Composer 13
Conductor 13
Creative team 15
  maintaing the vision 15
Cut tracks 135

D

Daily "in/out" sheet 133
Dance captain 5
  a day in the life of 141
  assistant dance captain 5, 13
  balancing the leadership aspect 151
  co-dance captain 5
  dance captain and choreographers 37
    handling conflict 41
    when to contact 42
  dance captains and stage managers 22
    dividing responsibilities 32
    working with different personalities: 33
  dance captains and swings 22
  definition 5
  extras to help you 161
  finding a support system 159
  offstage and onstage 35
  practise exercises 165

salary 12
the duties of 6
the expectations of 11
training you need 156
when a dance captain is hired 5
Dance supervisor 13, 19
Director 13
   assistant director 13
   associate director 13
   resident director 20

E

Equity required chorus calls 129
Equity's guidelines for dance captains 6

J

Job functions of co-workers 15
Job titles of co-workers 13, 15

L

Learning names quickly 165
Lift rehearsals 114
Lyricyst 13

M

Musical director 13, 20
   assistant musical director 13
   associate musical director 13
Musical staging 6
Musical supervisor 13, 20

N

Notes
   dealing with different personalities 48
   managing different personalities 49
   taking and giving 45
   ways to give notes 53
   when to give notes 51

O

Overtime 98

P

Partnering rehearsals 119
Practise exercises 165

creating cut tracks 169
eye for detail 168
figuring out what swings need 169
giving notes 168
learning names quickly 165
teaching 168
what would you do? 170
Props 34
Put-ins 107

Q

Quick rehearsal reference 161

R

Rehearsals 97, 157
   brush-up 114
   lift rehearsals 114
   overtime 98
   partnering rehearsals 119
   put-ins 107
   safety rehearsals 118
   weekly rehearsals 99
Resident choreographer 13, 19
Resident director 20
Running auditions 129

S

Safety rehearsals 118
Scheduling 121
Show bible 55
   charts 57
   choreography 75
   Stage Write 84
   staging notes 72
   Staging Score 88
   tracking sheets 80
   using recordings for bible 94
Stage manager 20
   assistant stage manager 13
   dance captains and stage managers 22
      dividing responsibilities 32
      working with different personalities 33
Stage Write 84
Staging notes 72
Staging Score 88
Stand-by 20
Swing 20

    dance captains and swings 22
    full swing 22
    partial swing 22
    universal swing 22
    vacation swing 22
Swing chart 161
Swing to-do list 163

T

Tracking sheets 80

U

Understudy 20

W

Weekly rehearsals 99
Weekly schedule 122
What Broadway people say makes the best dance captain 145

Printed in Great Britain
by Amazon